Bryan Webb's Kitchen

GRAFFEG

Published by Graffeg
First published 2008
Copyright © Graffeg 2008

Graffeg,
Radnor Court,
256 Cowbridge Road East,
Cardiff CF5 1GZ
Wales UK.
Tel: +44 (0)29 2037 7312
sales@graffeg.com
www.graffeg.com

Graffeg are hereby identified as the authors of this work in accordance with section 77 of the Copyrights, Designs and Patents Act 1988.

Distributed by the Welsh Books Council www.cllc.org.uk castellbrychan@cllc.org.uk

A CIP Catalogue record for this book is available from the British Library.

Designed and produced by Peter Gill & Associates
sales@petergill.com
www.petergill.com

**Tyddyn Llan Restaurant
with Rooms**
Llandrillo, nr. Corwen,
Denbighshire
LL21 0ST Wales UK
+44 (0)1490 440264
tyddynllan@compuserve.com
www.tyddynllan.co.uk

Bryan Webb's Kitchen.
Text © Bryan Webb 2008.

The publishers are also grateful to the Welsh Books Council for their financial support and marketing advice.
www.gwales.com

Every effort has been made to ensure that the information in this book is current and it is given in good faith at the time of publication. Please be aware that circumstances can change and be sure to check details before visiting any of the restaurants featured.

Photo credits
© Blas ar Fwyd: 153. © Bryan and Susan Webb: 16, 23, 25, 119, 147. © Crown copyright: 85. Harry Williams Photography: 8, 10, 11, 15, 26, 31, 32, 33, 36, 37, 40, 42, 43, 45, 46, 47, 50, 51, 59, 61, 62, 66, 69, 70, 72, 73, 74, 75, 76, 78, 79, 80, 81, 82, 84, 90, 92, 100, 103, 109, 113, 117, 120, 122, 126, 132, 133, 134, 136, 137, 139, 140, 143, 144, 148, 149, 152, 156, 157, 159, 173, 180, 185, 190, 191, 192, 193, 202, 204, 205, 208, 214. © Keltic Seafare: 155. © Liverpool Daily Post (photographers: Jeff Pitt; Stacey Roberts; Robert Parry Jones): 6, 9, 12, 27, 29, 35, 49, 52, 55, 57, 60, 63, 64, 65, 67, 87, 88, 90, 91,94, 95, 96, 99, 104, 107, 109, 111, 115, 127, 131, 134, 140, 146, 151, 160, 163, 165, 166, 169, 171, 172, 175, 177, 178, 181, 182, 184, 186, 188, 194, 195, 196, 198, 200, 201. © Nick Smith: 77, 125, 129, 130.

Thanks
I wish to thank my mum, without whose love and support Hilaire and Tyddyn Llan would still be a dream. I should also like to thank Susan for her love and encouragement when things did not go the way I had hoped, and for making the front of house operations so smooth and friendly.

My thanks also go to all my chefs past and present: Ian, Sweetie Petie, Jon, Denise, Jeremy, Steve, Cheeky Danny and Jason. And at Tyddyn Llan: Andrew, Berwyn, Siôn and James.

Thanks to Carol, for passing on her computer knowledge and putting up with the day-to-day hassle that I give her; to all the housekeeping and restaurant staff who have given Susan and I their great support since we arrived in North Wales.

A big thank you to my photographers at the Daily Post; to my publisher, Peter Gill, and to Vanessa – for all their help, and to Joana for her great design.

Thanks to Sarah Batley at the Daily Post for editing my weekly column, and to all my readers. Thank you to Igor and Ellen for pointing out the mistakes and compiling the index.

To our loyal customers at Tyddyn Llan, thank you for your support.

And finally I'd like to thank my late father, who pushed me to the extreme because he believed in me.

Thank you all

Bryan Webb

Bryan Webb's Kitchen

For my mum

GRAFFEG

Contents

Foreword

It was a great surprise and also an honour to be asked by Bryan to write the foreword to his first cookery book *Bryan Webb's Kitchen*. We have followed, with great enthusiasm, Bryan's career right from the beginning and seeing the shy young man go from strength to strength. We admired his tenacity, graft and love for his chosen career. We followed him to London when he left Wales, the country of his birth, where he eventually became the chef/proprietor of the highly acclaimed restaurant Hilaire on the Old Brompton Rd. We would in fact follow him anywhere just to eat his perfectly cooked grouse! My wife loves his lobster with coriander. Come to think of it, lobster followed by grouse - perfect! His food is honest and unpretentious. He cooks from his heart. The joy of eating Bryan's food stays with us for days. Now he is back in his beloved Wales, a trip to Tyddyn Llan - Restaurant with Rooms (which he bought a few years ago) is a must if we are anywhere in the vicinity. It is also worth a special trip. It is a pretty Georgian country house in a beautiful location. Here,

Bryan can find wonderful local produce on his doorstep; game and the freshest of fish, Welsh lamb and so on, which he prepares with great élan. I did once have a secret hope that he would buy my restaurant, The Walnut Tree near Abergavenny, when we came to the big decision to retire seven years ago. It was not to be as he settled for north Wales, to be precise Llandrillo, their gain!

We must not forget to mention Susan, Bryan's wife, who so ably supports him and is the ebullient face that welcomes you to this patch of culinary magic. A perfect foil to Bryan's shyness!

Enjoy this cookbook, it is written from his heart.

Franco Taruschio

Tyddyn Llan

Introduction

This cookbook had been planned in my head for a very long time. The title was always there, but the content only materialized after three years of writing my weekly column in the Daily Post.

When it comes to deadlines, I have always been tight; menus are never ready until minutes before customers arrive. Today, I am writing the introduction with the publication date right in front of me.

I have always believed that every chef's dream is to own their own restaurant; gain a Michelin star and write a cookbook. Well two out of three is Brian Webb's Kitchen. I have spent over 30 years cooking for a living, after leaving the Welsh valleys mining community.

Leaving home at the age of 16 I went to work for Sonia and Neville Blech who ran The Crown at Whitebrook, near Monmouth. What I hadn't appreciated at the time was just how good The Crown really was – it was the only Michelin starred restaurant in Wales. Sonia and Neville paved the road to what I have achieved as a chef and restaurateur.

I haven't always made the right decision during my career, such as the time I turned down a job at the Waterside Inn at Bray, with three Michelin stars. However, months later I was awarded the William Hepinstall award for young chefs and I took the opportunity to travel and work in France for a few months. I then moved to London as a head chef at the age of 24 – having worked at just three restaurants. Sometimes being young and naive helps.

This was the stepping stone for me to take over the kitchen two years later at Hilaire where after a buy out from the owners I stayed for 14 very happy years.

I have never worked in a large kitchen with an army of chefs. The most that ever help me at one time in the kitchen is three but with the style of food we serve we can cook for 50 à la carte meals with ease. My style has evolved over many years from reading books, eating in restaurants and following trends until I realized what style and direction I was happy with.

This book is a collection of recipes, ideas and memories that have helped make what Tyddyn Llan is today. The food we serve is simple and product led. I cook to please myself and my customers and not to achieve accolades. Of course when they are given it's fantastic, but a full and happy restaurant of guests is the most important thing in this life.

There is very little that I don't cook, like or eat and over a year through the seasons a wide range of my dishes will chop and change on my menus. I hope you enjoy my book, try the recipes and gain an insight to the food that Wales has to offer.

Bryan

The road back to Wales

Hilaire

After 14 years in a basement cupboard of a kitchen – you get less for killing your wife – I wanted a kitchen with a window and a view.

Tyddyn Llan

Ironically the weekend after we made the decision we went to stay at Tyddyn Llan for Easter. It only took one week to find a buyer,

After 14 years in a basement cupboard of a kitchen, I wanted a kitchen with a window and a view.

For many chefs 14 years in the same kitchen is unheard of, and the number of times I cleaned down my cooker at Hilaire at the end of service must have run into the thousands. Making the decision to sell Hilaire was one of the most difficult of my life. The idea was prompted by Susan. She put it all into perspective; the business was not improving and there were not sufficient funds to give Hilaire the face lift it needed. My main problem was the other major shareholder was dragging the whole show down and the only way to get rid of him was to sell. There were other reasons to sell and move on: reaching the age of 40; the street being overtaken with coffee shops; the ever-increasing rent demands; not to mention the feeling of becoming stale. So Susan and I took a chance and moved on.

but it took another three months of hell and negotiations to finalise the sale and as the time moved closer to the final service my emotions were becoming much more intense. One of the most difficult aspects of the sale was the day I had to inform the staff that a buyer for the restaurant had been found. Finding it hard to hold back the tears, I chose a moment when they were all together and as the words were leaving my mouth I could see the expressions on their faces. It all became too much and I retreated back into the kitchen.

Susan slowly but surely began telling all our regular customers the news. The most common reaction was 'Oh no! What are we going to do now? Where are we going to eat now?' Sometimes this was the reaction of customers who we saw only once or twice a year – well, surely that was one of the reasons! If I look back to 1987 when I took over from Simon Hopkinson, so many restaurants have come and gone and the only places of any size were Langans and the Caprice. Take a look at the restaurant trade in London now and, boy, how it has changed.

On 20th July Hilaire was packed with some of our most loyal customers and friends. It was a great evening full of mixed emotions and lots of memories. The evening had turned into early morning before we said a farewell to our regulars, all promising to trek to Wales to visit us. That night after my final service and the lights went out I locked the front door of Hilaire for the final time. Susan and I were now unemployed and unemployable.

south of Melbourne, that Wales was far more beautiful. We followed the coast from the Gower along to Fishguard and up to Cardigan Bay. At Machynlleth we could not find any accommodation so we found ourselves staying at Tyddyn Llan, near Corwen in Denbighshire, which was somewhere we had always liked. While there we discovered that Peter and Bridget were thinking of selling. We felt that in no way would we be able to raise the money or run a hotel for that matter. But after visiting the Yorke Arms, a hotel in Ramsgill which is run by a lovely couple, Frances and Bill Atkins, who used to run a restaurant on Old Brompton Road during the same years as us, we thought 'yes, we can do this!'. We were laughed at by quite a few banks during the summer.

We wanted Tyddyn Llan to be a destination for good food and wine

We did not head straight back to Wales but back via two world trips lasting eight months, during which time we decided where in Wales we would settle. Our first attempt to get back into business at the Gockett (a run-down pub near Monmouth) failed when we were gazumped at the last minute. At that point we had sold everything and moved to a small converted barn holiday let so we could be on hand during the renovations. So we started looking again. There were two things that we were 100 percent agreed on: that it had to be a freehold property and, after the bitter taste of a greedy investor at Hilaire, that no one else was to be financially involved. This limited our choice, but after viewing many properties I decided to take Susan on a coastal road tour of Wales. I had told her when we were driving along the Great Ocean Road

In August, after a quickly arranged meeting at Tyddyn Llan with a friendly bank manager called Shaun a deal was agreed. In November, we finally took over.

We had a bit of a shock in store when we took over as, apart from the second and only other chef in the kitchen disappearing on the opening night, running a hotel seemed so much more demanding than running a small restaurant on the Old Brompton Road.

Apart from the attraction of the natural beauty of North Wales, and despite the many things to do in the area, we wanted Tyddyn Llan to be a destination for good food and wine. Over the years my passion for finding wonderful ingredients has grown and, with my style of cooking, which on the surface seems simple but requires a lot of work and preparation, the end result is all about the taste.

HILAIRE'S LAST SUPPER JULY 20th

Pea and mint soup
Wild mushroom risotto
Tagliatelle with broad beans, bacon and mustard
Dressed crab vinaigrette and herbs
Griddled scallops, vegetable relish and rocket
Goujons of plaice with Thai dip
Smoked eel with new potatoes and bacon
Half lobster, mayonnaise or hot with chilli and lime butter +£5
Buffalo mozzarella, Piedmontese pepper and rocket
Parfait of foie gras and chicken livers with onion chutney

Roast sea bass with Laverbread "beurre blanc"
Char grilled turbot, pesto risotto and summer vegetables
Char grilled tuna, lentils, salsa verde and rocket
Wild salmon with asparagus salad
Grilled Dorset lobster with chilli, ginger and lime butter +£8
Breast of duck, potato pancake, port and blackcurrants
Fillet steak "au poivre"
Calves liver with beetroot, horseradish and fried sage
Rack of new seasons lamb, herb crust and gratin dauphinois

Trio of chocolates
Whimberry crème brûlée and sorbet
Summer pudding with Jersey cream
Port and blackcurrant jelly
Cherry and almond tart with vanilla ice cream
Strawberry shortbread with jersey cream
Tiramisù
Selection of ice creams and sorbets
British Farmhouse cheese from Neal's Yard

Please be understanding if certain dishes become unavailable

Three Courses £40.00 : Starter and Main Course £35.00
Two Starters £25.00 : Desserts £7.00 : Main Course only £24.00
Discretionary Service 12½% : Please No Pipes, Cigars or Mobile Phones

Travelling

Australia

Thailand

My wife has a passion for travelling. After eight months of living out of a suitcase I had had enough, but Susan could have gone on for ever, even though she had broken her knee while skiing and we had run out of money.

The master plan was to sell the house and restaurant in London, move everything to my home village of Crumlin where we had bought a house some three years previously and take a gap year travelling. Over the years we had employed many Australians and South Africans who worked in restaurants while making their way around the world and this had made us green with envy, as during our twenties we had never had the time to travel. But with no restaurant, job or huge mortgage we were free to go.

When the final day of service at Hilaire approached we were very excited about our forthcoming travels but had a feeling of utter loss and sadness at selling our way of life for the past 14 years. I had taken about two months to plan our trip and had driven the lady at the travel agents mad. But I knew what I wanted and picked away at the schedule until I got it right.

Scotland

We had a whole month to ourselves before we were due to fly to Australia and we had a lot to do as we were also selling our house in London. Our first mini trip was to south west Scotland to take our precious black cat, Tiger, to Betty and Rolston's in Newton Stewart. The trip to Scotland included some fine lunches and dinners.

Once the sale of our house had gone through and all our possessions were on the road to Wales, we had a farewell lunch at Restaurant Gordon Ramsay in Royal Hospital Road where Jean Claude treated us like king and queen.

We then took the train to South Wales ready to unpack our belongings and pack for our world adventure.

Thailand

First stop on the grand tour was the Oriental Hotel in Bangkok. We both love this hotel. It is just-affordable luxury and the food in all of their restaurants is to die for. Susan's favourite dish was a chicken and coconut soup, but the dressed crab with pawpaw and rock lobster with chilli and rock salt were delicious.

It had been a month now since we had left the hot kitchen of Hilaire, but walking around the streets of Bangkok you get the same feeling of heat. The markets in Bangkok blow you away with their assortments of different chillies, herbs and vegetables. You just have to gaze and look on with admiration, though I did buy some fish cakes from a street vendor which were delicious and a fraction of what you would pay for them back home.

Australia

With foot and mouth affecting the farming community back home, the Australians were taking no chances and the airport checks to enter Australia were very strict but nothing like what we have to go through at airports these days. Alison, our friend in Sydney, picked us up from the airport and we headed straight to the city centre. My first meal in Oz was their most common fish, barramundi, which we ate at a restaurant called Doyle's, outside in the sunshine overlooking the great harbour bridge. We had arrived but I had to pinch myself to realise that it was true.

I had worked with a few very good second chefs in London and three of them were living and working in Australia. Darren, who is native to the country, was working in Sydney at Celsius and we had a lunch reservation at his restaurant. But beforehand we had to tick off one of our 'to do' boxes by climbing over the Sydney Harbour Bridge. It was breathtaking. The lunch was excellent, too, with Darren looking after us, and a stunning terrine of aubergine, tomato and goats' cheese sticks out in my memory.

All the meals we had during our ten days in Sydney were very good, but I must admit that we did not understand Tetsuya's – where East meets West but gets lost in the process. Rockpool was amazing, I can still remember the John Dory with spices and Indian bread. Probably the best restaurant was one called Banc, which was set in a former bank building. It had a very elegant dining room, and the food was so good that on the day I set my alarm clock early in order to visit the famous fish market at the crack of dawn, I took myself off for lunch there on my own. It's not something I do regularly, but it was a way of studying more closely both the food and the way the service was run. As for the market – what an interesting place. I was expecting something like Billingsgate, but with the way the fish was auctioned it was fascinating. The one question I had to ask was what was in the cement mixers? They used them to tenderise octopus, I was told. Well, that was a new one on me.

absence she could run the kitchen with ease. She always knew what I was thinking even before I thought it. Just brilliant. Being an excellent cook, we ate at home quite a lot, so my first meal out was fish and chips. This is as much Aussie food as British, but they do it better. First, there's the fish shop, laid out like one of our fish mongers. You choose your fish, then how you want it cooked: battered or bread-crumbed, deep fried or plain grilled. Amazing. I'm sure it's done in this country now but at the time I felt it was a great concept.

We ate out a few times and the one dish that was so simple it still takes me back was deep fried king prawns, or even yabbies, coated in coconut and macadamia nuts. It was crisp, fresh and a delight. The other meal we will never forget, but for all the wrong reasons, was at the Versace hotel, where Thierry is the food and beverage manager. The meal was first class and impressively cooked by a fellow Welshman, but the date was 9/11, and when we arrived back home and Thierry was flicking through the channels, we saw the Twin Towers and a plane crashing into one of them. With full bellies, and plenty of wine, it was even harder to accept, though obviously after a night's sleep it was reality.

The airports had calmed down by the next flight. Security was high but we both felt safe, which was just as well as we had another

The one question I had to ask was what was in the cement mixers? They used them to tenderise octopus, I was told.

We flew in to Brisbane to visit my longstanding second chef Denise and her French husband Thierry who moved out a few years back. Denise is a great chef. In my

26 flights to go. Melbourne was the home to cheeky Danny who worked in our kitchens for many years. It was always his dream to live in Australia. Danny was working for Donovan

Cooke, the ex-head chef of three-starred Marco Pierre White. The food was very Marco.

The place that really impressed us was coincidentally called Donovan's, on the coast at St Kilda. Although it was late winter during our visit, we still appreciated the stylish concept of eating and drinking by the sea. The place had a homely feel to it; so relaxing. It gave us plenty to think about in terms of what we would like to do on our return home if we were finally to go for the Gockett pub. The food at Donovan's had an Italian slant, with lots of fish.

a glass of wine at 11.30 in the morning. Well, in our defence, we were in one of Australia's best wine regions.

Australia is a huge country, but sometimes you get the feeling that it is such a small world. When we stayed at a charming cottage in Robe we flicked though the visitors' book and discovered that Jo, another Aussie chef who worked in the kitchens of Hilaire, had stayed in the same house only a few weeks before. From Robe we indulged Susan's passion of checking out lighthouses, right along the coast toward Adelaide where we were to meet up

We left Donovan's in awe of the place and bursting with ideas.

Their classic take on fish and chips was wrapped in greaseproof paper made to look like a sheet of newspaper – a very nice touch. We left Donovan's in awe of the place and bursting with ideas.

We took two days to travel along the Great Ocean Road. The sights were breathtaking but there was nothing gastronomic about the food. Before arriving in Australia, I had dreamed of standing on the platform of the now-closed down railway station at Coonawarra, South Australia, just like the publicity shots of Kym Tolley of Penley wines. I finally got to do that, striking the pose in a beanie (bobble hat to you and me). We arrived at Penola with time to spare before our agreed meeting at the winery, so made our way to a recommended restaurant, Pipers, where the tapas was supposed to be great, for some lunch. What we had failed to realise is that we had driven into a different time zone and so were 30 minutes early for everything. Small wonder they were not ready when we rocked up at the restaurant and looked at us strangely when we requested

with Kym Tolley at the offices of Penley's. Kym treated us to a delicious lunch which was washed down with Penley's Riesling and Cabernet Sauvignon. One great wine discovery in Adelaide was Rockford Basket Press. We were out to dinner at the Universal wine bar with relations of another Australian chef who had worked for us, and they ordered the wine. It soon became a mission to put it onto my wine list.

Adelaide is a great city, mainly arranged in blocks (the natives appear scared stiff of driving around the few roundabouts that do exist). The other dining experiences there were the Citrus, which offered light and modern food, and a restaurant in the Hilton run by Cheong Liew who cooked some excellent French fusion food that worked and which I really enjoyed. But you should not leave the town without trying a pie floater: a meat pie topped with mushy peas and brown sauce wrapped in paper from the pie van.

Driving though the beautiful Barossa Valley north of Adelaide we stopped off at Rockford,

New Zealand

Visiting vineyards
and meeting
the wine masters
continued to play
a big part in our
journey

New Zealand

We spent two weeks
covering many miles
around the country in
a camper van.

Penfold's and to see how the big boys do it at Jacob's Creek. We lunched at Maggie Beer's café and stayed at a country house called The Hermitage which made for an excellent day. The next plan was to visit Streaky Bay, a small village on the coast where the parents of Jason, the last second chef at Hilaire, had invited us to stay for a weekend. This is when you realise how big a country it really is. It took us two days of driving, with a night in a motel where I was refused BYO in the country that invented it. The following day I was stopped by the police for speeding, the first time ever, and by the time we had arrived in Streaky Bay and paid the fine the whole place knew we had arrived.

New words were learnt at this far remote village: 'snags', 'grog' and some good 'tucker' were had by all and, as for Bring Your Own, when you are invited to a barbie in this town you take your own steaks, 'snags' and beer. During our short stay we were treated like royalty and shown some wonderful places, though the bugs were out to get Susan.

The last part of our Australian adventure was to visit Alice Springs, Kings Canyon and Ayers Rock, which we walked around, climbed on top of and flew over in a helicopter. Food in this part of Australia is what you would expect from tourist destinations, and we went the whole hog by taking the 'Sounds of Silence' dinner where you eat out in the desert under the stars and the moon. It was an amazing experience, including some Australian delicacies. I discovered that crocodile was not for me.

New Zealand

The next day we headed back to Alice Springs for the flight to New Zealand and it was only as we were leaving that I realised that the only kangaroos I had seen had either been on a farm, dead on the road side or else on my plate – and, yes, it's very tasty in Australia.

New Zealand has very similar scenery to Wales, and plenty of sheep. Our first destination on arrival was Auckland, where lunch and dinner was so cheap once you realised that you were getting four dollars to the pound. We spent two weeks covering many miles around the country in a camper van, although with my well-known skill at anything unrelated to cooking the first few days were a trying time. Topping up with water and emptying the waste I made Mr Bean look intelligent, but I soon got the hang of things. Over the two weeks I cooked some tasty meals, though cooking fish in such a small van and then having to sleep in it overnight is not recommended. Another day we stopped to make lunch, and Susan washed up but left the pans and plates to dry on the draining board, next to a sink full of dirty water. You can imagine the mess when we drove off!

We travelled to the very tip of North Island and across South Island to Christchurch and I would recommend it to anyone. Only once, in Wellington, did we succumb to the thought of luxury, staying the night in a hotel. Well, there were no camp sites in the town anyway. Of all my food memories in New Zealand, the ones that stick out were firstly the prawns that we bought at a prawn farm which was educational in itself. They were simply fried in the camper van, served over some freshly boiled asparagus and dressed with a Thai fish sauce with a hint of chilli. The other memory was the best fish and chips which we found in a harbour called Akaroa tucked away near Christchurch. I don't know why, but they were amazing.

Visiting vineyards and meeting the wine masters continued to play a big part in our journey and it was a huge thrill when we drove down the drive to Cloudy Bay, the most famous winery in New Zealand and from which a huge trend began.

China

Flying out of New Zealand to our next destination, Beijing, I began to feel like a timelord. We left at 6.30am, arrived in Sydney at 6.45am, then flew via Hong Kong, finally arriving at Beijing at 10pm – a total travelling time of 24 hours. Boy, I was pleased when I collected the luggage and saw a smart Chinese man waving a card with 'Mr Webb' on it. With all our luggage in it the boot would not close, but at this point it did not matter. I just wanted him to drive and show us a bed.

For many years Susan and I had wanted to see the Seven Wonders of the World, and in this gap year we were finally going to tick them all off the list. Already ticked off were the Grand Canyon, Acropolis, Taj Mahal, and Ayers Rock. There were three to go, and the Great Wall of China was next. It was a breathtaking sight and there were only a few tourists to be seen in the part we were taken to. Susan and I walked and walked, so enthralled by this magnificent masterpiece, although we probably walked too far as the guide was pretty sharp on our return to base.

Beijing is an amazing place but not one that I would visit without a guide, as it can be pretty intense. I have always been a lover of Chinese cuisine and I was raring to sample it in its native home. I had only eaten it in the Chinatowns of London and Manchester and it took some getting used to, even for my cast iron stomach. After a visit to the Beijing Opera a banquet of Peking Duck was first class.

Shanghai was our next stop and there I was intrigued watching the ladies making dim sum in the restaurant windows. I had to try them. As we were the only British people in the place and the menu was in Chinese, we just pointed and I will always remember this dumpling with a straw sticking out of it. When you sucked, it tasted like pure pork fat. Some authentic pork-wrapped won tons, chopped chicken and sticky rice set me up in more ways than one.

In the city of Xian I asked to visit a market, and on a Sunday morning we set off to see one. The array of produce was amazing: all sizes of squid and cuttlefish, live turtles (which surprised me), live chickens, sausages, pork and huge displays of vegetables. The Chinese must work so hard because a number of them were sleeping on their stalls while waiting for customers. With the smell from the market starting to get to me, and the previous day's dim sum still making themselves felt, we set off to see the Terracotta Army, which was one of the highlights I was looking forward to. Squeeze tight, I thought to myself, and everything will be all right. The warriors were an amazing discovery and will stay in my memory for ever, but for the rest of the China visit I have to confess I stuck to club sandwiches and pizza.

We then flew to Guilin with Air China, an airline whose safety message might have read 'if we crash, you die'. But we landed safely and there, on the Lijiang River, we watched a very different style of fishing, with cormorants catching the fish in their mouths. On the trip we were offered a glass of wine, but having already sampled a bottle or two of Great Wall of China wine, I decided that this one was going too far. It was snake wine with the snake still in the bottle. I said 'No, thanks,' but Susan had a glass. That girl would drink anything to prove a point!

China

China

I have always been a
lover of Chinese cuisine
and I was raring to
sample it in its native
home. I had only eaten
it in the Chinatowns of
London and Manchester
and it took some getting
used to, even for my cast
iron stomach.

Hong Kong

Hong Kong was always a place I had wanted to visit since the late 80s when Hilaire's restaurant manager Dominic Ford moved there to open a bar at the Mandarin Hotel. I had wanted to go out to visit, but before I could make the trip he was back developing Harvey Nichols' food and beverage operations. We arrived late on Halloween and in the hotel bar a party was in full swing. The next day we took the Star Ferry over to Kowloon, where we visited markets and did the sights. I wasn't sure if I liked the place, but the food was more of the style to which I had grown accustomed. I did get to the Mandarin Oriental Hotel, and the dinner there was amazing, if slightly expensive even for Hong Kong standards.

That marked the end of our first trip during our gap year, and we returned home to our house in Wales. But not even a week passed before we were off again, this time to Egypt to cross the Pyramids off the list of Seven Wonders. Foodwise, this was not the country. Only one meal sticks out and that was an Indian at the Mena House Hotel, for which my mum paid, and of which she only ate a spoonful of boiled rice.

New York

The year 2001 marked Susan's 40th birthday and a party was duly organised at home with 24 guests sitting down to lunch of parfait of foie gras and chicken livers, pumpkin soup, chicken with morels, followed by a trio of chocolates – all requested by Susan. The big day itself was December 8th and we were in Susan's favourite city, New York. It was good to see that the city had kept its dignity and was in good spirits after 9/11. Its people were very friendly and the restaurants on fine form.

The whole point of the second part of the world tour was to do it as cheaply as possible, staying with old Hilaire customers at various points of the journey and cooking for them at dinner parties. The first couple, Henry and Sandy, have since become great friends with us returning many times to their home at Milford on the sound in Connecticut. We cooked three dinners at their house and it was just so much fun. Henry's Martini cocktails are legendary and extremely powerful. During our visit they took us to New Haven, Connecticut, the home of Yale University where many presidents, and of course Henry, studied. What really did get my attention was Louis' Lunch, the home of the hamburger where they are served in-between two slices of toasted bread, with no chips, and no nonsense; just great tasting burgers.

Our next dinner party was with Janice and Lane at their Mansion in Greenwich, Connecticut, two customers who always visited us when in London. This was to be a more formal affair with Susan serving and me in the kitchen where I belong. Janice knew what she wanted and I remember it was the first time for a very long time that I had made puff pastry. Our trip continued with us visiting upstate New York via Saratoga Springs and then going onto Niagara to see the Falls, thereby crossing off the last of our Seven Wonders of the World. Christmas was spent skiing and cooking for our hosts and friends at Whistler, British Columbia, where on the last day of the last downhill run something happened that changed our plans somewhat: Susan fell and broke her knee. It meant I had to push her around Seattle and California in a wheelchair, which I think she actually became accustomed to in the end.

L.A.

I cooked for our biggest foodie friend Mike, and his wife Pat, in L.A. where the choice of ingredients would blow anyone away. They really were into their food as were their guests. Who says the Americans don't like great food?

Japan

From L.A. we travelled onto Tokyo, via Hawaii where we celebrated our wedding anniversary with a week on the beach and seeing the sights. It's amazing what treatment you get when you're in a wheelchair or hobbling on crutches. It was late in the day on our arrival in Tokyo and I tried to order food in a noodle bar, which ended up with me pointing at pictures in the window. At 5am I was wide awake and, as one of my ambitions was to visit the Tokyo fish market, it seemed to be the right day. Susan wanted to come too, so we put the wheelchair in the back of the cab and off we went. The atmosphere was electric. I had never seen such a busy place. It was pretty frightening for Susan being pushed around the cobbled pathways in-between the stalls with motorised trolleys zooming in and out of them. It's an unbelievable place even before your eyes have seen the magnificent displays of fish: rows and rows of tuna and species totally unknown to me. Even the vegetable market was something else.

Our trip to Japan had to be cut short, and the South African part cancelled, due to Susan's knee which needed real attention now, not to mention the fact that due to our habit of staying in good hotels and eating our way around the world our finances were in a poor state. But there was still time for a curry at the Tiffin Room and a Singapore Sling at Raffles before we headed home to reality and our quest to open up a restaurant business again.

Hong Kong

Japan

Avocado

The avocado is a rather bizarre fruit, since instead of getting sweeter as it ripens it develops a very high fat content. They are also unusual among fruits in being able to ripen only when they are off the tree.

Avocados are native to the tropics of Central America. There are hundreds of varieties but if you can go for the Hass avocado – it is usually ideal. Avocado and prawns are as classic as the cocktail, but serving an under-ripe avocado with defrosted little pink commas and bottled mayo would be enough to put you off for life. My salsa is similar to Guacamole and is good eaten on its own with some pitta bread. If you ever find yourself in Santa Monica, C.A. head for the Boarder Grill on 3rd Street for the best Guacamole ever.

Avocado is a bizarre fruit, it develops a very high fat content as it ripens.

Avocado salsa and langoustine cocktail

Ingredients

32 cooked langoustines or large prawns
8 cherry tomatoes
Heart of a good lettuce
4 ripe avocados
1 small red pepper in very small dice
1 finely chopped onion, small dice
1 red chilli finely chopped
6 tablespoons of roughly chopped coriander
Juice of 2 limes
Salt and pepper
100ml olive oil

Serves 4

1 Peel the avocados and remove the stones but keep them to one side.

2 Mash the avocado with a potato masher.

3 Add the pepper, onion, chilli, coriander, lime juice mix all together.

4 Season with salt and pepper and stir in the olive oil. Put the stones back into the mixture, this stops it decolouring, cover with cling film and store until needed.

5 Arrange some shredded lettuce in the bottom of four glasses with the halved cherry tomatoes; add a tablespoon of salsa and seven prawns to each glass.

6 Top with some more salsa and garnish with a prawn on top.

7 Any left over salsa goes well with cold chicken.

Roast chicken

Roast Chicken makes a perfect and affordable roast Sunday dinner at home, and the best part for a greedy chef like me is picking at the wings and carcass and the oyster from the undercarriage – for me the perfect comfort food and the thing I crave for on holiday.

For this recipe I suggest legs of chicken – after the oyster my favourite part – but for some reason it does not sell too well in the restaurant, maybe two portions compared to twenty portions of beef on a Sunday lunch. People prefer the breast for some reason, but for flavour I'm a leg man. The dried morels in the sauce are very expensive and are available in supermarkets, but you can use other mushrooms or just leave them out. You can prepare this dish in advance and reheat, it makes a splendid dinner with spinach, mashed potato or with a potato pancake.

for me the perfect comfort food and the thing I crave for on holiday.

chicken with tarragon
and morels

Ingredients

4 large chicken legs or breasts

125ml glass of sweet white wine

125ml glass of dry sherry

50g dried morels, soaked in a little cold water
    and cut in half. Save the water.

500ml of chicken stock

500ml double cream

Fresh picked tarragon

3 tablespoons sunflower oil

Potato pancake mixture (see page 194)

100g cooked spinach

Salt and pepper

Serves 4

1 In a large pan big enough to hold all the chicken, heat the oil and place the legs in the pan skin side down and fry until golden brown. Turn and season with salt and pepper, remove from the pan and discard the oil.

2 Add the wine and sherry and let it boil for a few minutes. Put the chicken back in and cover with the stock and morel water, bring to a simmer and cook for 30 minutes (10 to 12 minutes for breasts).

3 Remove the legs from the pan and boil the juices until reduced by half, add the cream and boil (be careful it does not boil over) until the sauce thickens slightly. Strain the sauce into a clean container and back into the pan. Add the chicken and the morels.

4 When ready to serve add the fresh tarragon.

5 Cook four potato pancakes and the spinach.

6 Place a pancake onto each plate, top with spinach and lay a chicken leg on top. Spoon the sauce over and around.

Thailand

One of my favourite beach holidays is in Thailand. Not only for the sun but because the food is fantastic, from fish cakes from a street stall to Chicken and Coconut Soup at the Oriental in Bangkok – my wife's favourite soup and hotel.

Many years ago I bought the best Thai cookbook, *Thai Cooking* by Jennifer Brennan. My copy is now falling apart, but if you come across it I strongly recommend that you buy it. Unfortunately North Wales does not have many Thai restaurants, but with some careful shopping and a few store cupboard essentials, such as Thai fish sauce (the squid variety is best), red and green curry paste, coconut milk in tins, together with rice and noodles, Thai food is easy to cook at home and will taste quite authentic.

These days fresh chillies, coriander, ginger and limes are available in the supermarkets; but if you know of an oriental grocers look out for lime leaves, galangal and lemon grass. All these will keep in the fridge for a couple of weeks, until you get the urge to try some Thai cooking.

For the goujons with Thai Dip, the trick to it is the breadcrumbs. We buy Japanese breadcrumbs, called Panko, from an oriental supermarket, and dust the fish strips in flour, then egg wash, and finally coat them in Panko. You can use any firm, white fish such as cod, hake or plaice and the same applies to making Thai-style Fishcakes.

To make Thai Fishcakes, take one pound of white fish, two tablespoons of red curry paste, one egg, two teaspoons of fish sauce, the juice and grated zest of one lime with a handful of coriander, whiz it up in a food processor until smooth, then shape into small cakes. Cover them with flour and deep fry until golden, serving with Thai Dip or a cucumber salad (one cucumber peeled, seeded and cut into small dice, two red chilli peppers seeded and chopped, two shallots chopped, two tablespoons of fish sauce, the juice of half a lime, mixed together and served).

Chicken and coconut soup

Ingredients

1200ml coconut milk (3 cans)
4 large chicken breasts cut into small pieces
3 spring onions, chopped
1 handful of coriander leaves, chopped,
4 red chillies chopped
Juice of 2 limes
200g button mushrooms quartered and
   cooked in a little butter
3 tablespoons fish sauce
1 tablespoon of red curry paste

Serves 6

1 In a saucepan, heat the coconut milk with the red curry paste.

2 Add the chicken pieces and simmer for 10 minutes, do not cover as this will curdle the milk.

3 Add the lime juice, spring onions, mushrooms, fish sauce and chillies.

4 Finally add the coriander and serve.

Goujons of cod with Thai dip

This is fun food, great as a starter, canapé or a light snack supper. It's also a good way of using small pieces of fish.

Ingredients

1 fillet of cod or plaice cut into thin strips,
   I like to serve between six and eight as
   a portion.
Panko breadcrumbs
2 eggs
Plain flour
Salt and pepper
Add chopped coriander before serving

Serves 6

1 Beat the eggs in a large bowl, season the flour with salt and pepper, place the strips of fish into the flour, then dip into the egg, carefully lift out and coat with the breadcrumbs. Lay on a tray until needed.

2 Heat a deep fryer to 180°C, fry the goujons in the fryer for a few minutes until crisp and golden, season with salt and serve straight away with the dip.

Thai dip

Ingredients

2 cloves of garlic
2 red chillies
1 teaspoon of sugar
Juice of two limes
3 tablespoons of water
3 tablespoons of fish sauce

1 Chop the chillies (leave the seeds in if you want extra kick), finely grate the garlic and mix with all the other ingredients in a small bowl. This keeps for up to two weeks in the fridge, but make sure it is well covered otherwise everything will have the taste of Thailand.

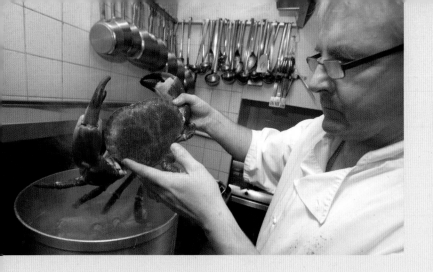

Crab

Crabs are mainly caught in baited pots that are laid on the sea floor and pulled in every now and again to be emptied. When buying a live crab, firstly make sure that it is actually alive. Look at its feet and shell. If the toes are well worn or if the shell has signs of barnacles then the crab will not have moulted recently and is likely to be fuller and meatier inside. Be careful if you buy cooked crabs, as you do not know if they were alive when cooked, or how long ago they were cooked. Go by your sense of smell and you can easily tell if it's not fresh.

Many people think that hen crabs are sweeter, but if you are going to dress a crab I think it wiser to go for a male cock crab, whose claws and body are fuller and easier to clean. The hen crab is generally smaller but, to distinguish between the two, examine the tail on the underside: the female is broader. This is where she keeps her eggs. Use hen crabs on plateaux of seafood or if you are going to pick and eat the crab at the table with a generous pot of mayonnaise.

For all its charm, dressing a crab is a time consuming job. You'll need picks, bowls and patience. It helps to have a few glasses of wine to hand and someone to share the job and talk with. If you have small crabs and want to dress them back in the shell, first pick all the meat out of the body and claws, keeping the brown and white meat separate, then deal with the shell. Look at the opened side and you will notice a fine line around the outer rim. Crack and tap along this line to knock away the inner, upper layer, making a neat crab shell bowl to serve the crab. Mash the brown meat with a fork and add a dash of Tabasco sauce and a drop of lemon juice, spoon this into the centre of each shell and fill the space either side with the white meat. You can also decorate it with lines of chopped hard boiled egg and chopped chives and parsley.

To cook crabs at home you will need a large saucepan of water, a peeled and chopped onion, a carrot and three sticks of celery, a few parsley stalks, bay leaves, a sprig of thyme, salt and a few peppercorns. A friend of mine says that the water should be as salty as the sea, so be generous with the salt. It's best to kill the crab before cooking it and a practical and humane way to do this is to insert a strong knife though the middle of the body under the tail, then plunge the crab into the boiling water. Bring to the boil and simmer for five minutes, then switch off and leave for 15 minutes. Remove from the pot and leave to cool before picking.

Dressed crab vinaigrette
with herbs

Ingredients

White meat from a 1½-2kg crab
4 large tablespoons of avocado salsa
1 tablespoon of chopped herbs
   (chives, parsley, tarragon and chervil)
Juice of half lemon
2 tablespoons of extra virgin olive oil
Mixed salad

For the sauce

brown meat from the crab
1 tablespoon of tomato ketchup
½ tablespoon of Dijon mustard
½ tablespoon of horseradish sauce
Juice of half lemon
2 anchovy fillets
2 teaspoons of brandy
Salt and pepper

Serves 4

1 Mix the crab meat with the herbs, lemon juice and olive oil, season with salt and pepper.

2 Purée all the sauce ingredients in a blender and pass though a fine sieve.

3 Place a pastry cutter in the centre of four plates and put a tablespoon of avocado salsa into each one. Fill the cutters with the crab meat. Remove the cutter.

4 Put three teaspoons of sauce around and decorate with a little salad.

Morocco

I had always wanted to go to Morocco, mainly to discover what its food was all about. I especially wanted to go after a customer said to my wife a few years ago after eating a Moroccan style lamb dish that she thought the chef had never been to Morocco. She was right, of course, though after my visit I don't think my recipe will change.

We really enjoyed the food in Marrakech but, even after eating in the best restaurant in town, it seemed to lack the wow factor that I was looking for. Chicken and lamb are the two main meats that Moroccans eat, either served as a tagine or as a part of a couscous. The salads they serve at the beginning of a meal are mouthwatering and challenge the taste buds.

Couscous is the national dish of North African countries such as Morocco; it is of Berber origin and is a truly local dish with many variations to the stew that accompanies it. Couscous itself is a type of fine semolina made from wheat grain; years ago Moroccan families would send wheat, which they would have bought at the market, to the local mill to be ground to the degree of fineness they preferred. Today it is bought ready-made, and is available at all supermarkets.

The grains of couscous are steamed over a stew or broth in a pot called a couscousier, which is like a double boiler. It is then served with the meat and vegetables and the sauce spiced up with some harissa in a separate jug. I don't see that there is much difference between a couscous stew and a tagine, it's more to do with the pot it's cooked in.

I had always wanted to go to Morocco

Moroccan chicken

Ingredients

8 small chicken legs

2 small onions, finely chopped

4 cloves of garlic, finely chopped

2.5cm of fresh ginger, peeled and finely
   chopped

1 tablespoon of coriander seeds, finely ground

A pinch of saffron

1 small tin of chick peas

6 preserved lemons, quartered

16 green olives, with the stones removed

125ml glass of white wine

500ml chicken stock

Olive oil

Salt and pepper

Serves 4

1 In a large casserole dish heat some olive oil and fry the chicken legs until golden brown in small batches, season with salt and pepper, and remove to a tray.

2 Add a little more oil and fry the onions, garlic and ginger until soft, add the coriander seeds and fry until they give off an aroma, pour in the wine and boil for a few minutes then add the chicken back into the pan, cover with chicken stock, add the pinch of saffron and simmer until cooked.

3 Now add the drained chick peas, lemons and olives, cook for a further 10 minutes, remove the chicken and keep warm while you reduce the sauce slightly, then pour over the chicken and serve. You could also add some dried apricots, dates and almonds if you wish. I would serve this with some steamed couscous sprinkled with chopped mint.

U.S.A.

Every time I go to America and see braised short ribs on a menu I must order it. Chez Panisse in Berkeley served it once with creamed polenta and braised radicchio; Daniel Boulud in New York pairs the succulent short rib with a rare slice of fillet. They are both good dishes.

I have never seen braised short ribs on a menu in this country. Maybe the reason is that it's not a cut that is readily available. For a long time I didn't know which cut I needed to reproduce the dish until my great butcher in Bala told me that in British butchery it is called Jacob's Ladder. It's a cut that comes from the brisket of beef and there are usually twelve ribs to a whole ladder, which then need to be cut in half lengthways. This dish takes a while to prepare and is best prepared a day in advance so the fats float to the top and set and can then easily be removed. It is a very cheap cut of meat that has such as great flavour, it just needs a lot of love and care in preparation.

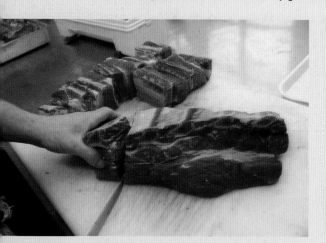

Jacob's Ladder

Braised short ribs of beef

Ingredients

4 short ribs of beef

1 large onion, finely chopped

3 carrots, finely chopped

4 sticks of celery, chopped

1 bouquet garni with bay leaves, parsley
  stalks, thyme and rosemary

Sunflower oil

1 bottle of red wine

500ml chicken stock

500ml veal stock

Salt and pepper

20 small onions

10 brown cap mushrooms, quartered

4 slices of streaky bacon cut into lardons
  (strips)

50g butter

25g flour

Serves 4

1 In a large saucepan heat some oil and gently brown the pieces of short ribs until golden, season and remove to a tray. Do this in batches so that you do not crowd the pan.

2 Add the vegetables and cook until soft and slightly coloured. Add the red wine and boil for five minutes to remove the raw alcohol, add the bouquet garni and the two stocks, cover with cold water and bring to a simmer. Skim off the scum (it will keep on rising so keep a watchful eye over the pot as it simmers away). Cook for about two and a half hours until the meat is tender and starts to fall away off the bone.

3 Leave to cool until the following day.

4 Remove the fats that will have become solid and gently reheat the pot. When warm carefully remove the ribs and then strain the sauce though a fine sieve into a clean saucepan. Reduce the sauce until it starts to thicken (this can be tricky as the sauce can become too strong in flavour). If you want a slightly thick sauce and not too strong it's best to add some beurre marnier (25g of butter and 25g flour mixed together). Add a little at a time until you get the desired consistency.

5 Add the ribs back to the sauce to reheat them but try not to boil the sauce.

6 In a separate saucepan add 25g of butter and slowly cook the onions with the strips of bacon until lightly brown and soft. Add the mushrooms and cook until tender. Drain away the excess butter and add the short ribs.

7 Serve two pieces each with some creamy mash or polenta.

Madness at

It took weeks for the realization to set in that our dream to buy the Gockett had fallen through. Mornings would arrive and there would be a feeling of 'what was the point?' But there had to be one.

While waiting at the doctors one day, Susan and I had a bet who could get a job first. We both immediately filled out application forms to work at a local five star hotel and I also joined an agency. Susan had a reply and, within days, an interview and an offer followed of a job as a food and beverage associate – in other words a waitress of the lowest level. Just before Susan started I also had a call to arrange an interview with the head chef of the same hotel, and meanwhile many calls came in from the agency, none of which were to my liking.

It's always a strange feeling walking into a new kitchen, but for me this was the first time I had done so in 14 years. The kitchen was huge but where were the staff? A chef introduced himself and I took it that he was the head man, so I took my orders and put my head down to whatever they wanted me to cook. I was impressed with the other chef as he seemed to be making hundreds of Yorkshire puddings and they were all perfect, not like my efforts at home on a Sunday roast. After about one hour a man of over 25 stone in weight appeared. He was the head chef and these were his last two days. There were three functions that day and by the end of it, having spent 12 hours on my feet, boy, were they aching.

It's always a strange feeling walking into a new kitchen, but for me this was the first time I had done so in 14 years.

I did two days at the five star establishment and was impressed at the organization of the place. There were in the region of 50 chefs and around 10 department head chefs. It was amazing but after my small kitchen at Hilaire I knew it was not for me. Susan took the job, winning the bet, and when the agency next called I took the first job offered.

I was supposed to work at the Manor in Crickhowell for two days but I ended up staying three months. I must say in a funny way I did enjoy my time there. I had free range to cook whatever I wanted on the menus, and tried to improve the functions. But what they were serving is what people wanted, just as long as there was lots of it. I could not believe it

the manor

I was determined that the last weekend would go well. I must say my 200 Yorkshire puddings rose and we did not run out of potatoes.

the first time I cooked this huge amount of vegetables and potatoes and we still ran out. I had a theory that they stuffed themselves silly, washed it down with plenty of alcohol, jiggled it all about on the dance floor but how they kept it all down was beyond me.

Saturdays were always big wedding days and, no matter how organised it all was, a spanner would be thrown in the works and there would be trouble. There were children's meals ordered with chips when you could not have the fryer on at the same time as the two ovens; there was the vegetarian who only ate chicken; the wedding party which turned up two hours early, and the constant call for more potatoes.

Staff turnover at any hotel or restaurant can be high but here it was quite alarming. I counted 10 people leaving within my first three weeks, and towards the end of my time at the Manor Hotel I became the longest serving chef – well, the only one, actually. By now I had roped my wife into being my assistant after the owner of the Manor, Glyn asked if she could cook. She can't but she

will listen, and she wasn't bad, either. She even made a dessert of trifle for a wedding and the bride pronounced it the best part of the meal. On my last week a new head chef started. I showed him how I had been doing things for the past few months and prepared him for what happened at the weekends. He seemed keen, so I took the Thursday off. When I arrived on the Friday morning he had gone. He'd quit after the lunch service on Thursday. I felt guilty about leaving, but I was determined that the last weekend would go well. I must say my 200 Yorkshire puddings rose and we did not run out of potatoes. At the very least I learnt there what the Taffs like.

The food for weddings at the Manor Hotel was very simple. Well, to be honest it had to be considering the volume of customers – up to 200 at one wedding and all sitting down at the same time – and the fact that there were only two in the kitchen to serve it. Simple food served well can sometimes be the best and the classic wedding menu would be: leek and potato soup, roast beef and Yorkshire pudding followed by trifle – these dishes, of course,

are as we would prepare them at Tyddyn Llan.
In fact every Sunday since we have been at
Tyddyn Llan we have roasted a sirloin of beef.
As the days run into each other making the
Yorkshire pudding mix reminds me which
day it is.

Simple food served well can be the best and
the classic wedding menu would be: leek and
potato soup, roast beef and Yorkshire pudding
followed by trifle.

Leek and potato soup

Ingredients

1 onion, finely chopped
4 leeks, white parts only cleaned and chopped
2 small potatoes peeled and diced
75g unsalted butter
1½ litres chicken stock or water
Salt and pepper

Serves 6

1 Melt the butter in a large pan and add the onions. Cook for about 5 minutes until soft. Do let them colour.

2 Add the leeks and season with salt and pepper, stir well and place a lid on the saucepan. Make sure that it's on a low heat, and gently cook in its own steam until the leeks are soft.

3 Add the stock and potatoes and gently simmer until the potato is well cooked.

4 Purée in a liquidizer and pass through a sieve, check the seasoning before serving.

Yorkshire pudding

Ingredients

4 eggs
250g plain flour
400ml milk
Salt and pepper
Dash of white wine vinegar

Makes 12

1 Sieve the flour into a large bowl, put the eggs into a small bowl and mix. Pour into the flour with a little of the milk and mix well. Add the milk and whisk to a smooth batter, add the salt and pepper and vinegar and pour though a sieve into a clean bowl.

2 Leave to rest for least two hours.

Roast beef and Yorkshire pudding

Ingredients

2kg piece of beef sirloin (preferably
  Welsh Black)
300ml glacé (see page 206)
1 glass of red wine (125ml)
A bunch of watercress
Salt and pepper

Serves 8

To roast the beef

I always find that it is best to bone out along
the centre bone down to the ribs, a technique
called shinning but leaving the meat attached
to the rib bone (your butcher will do this for
you). Trim away the sinew but keep to roast
with the joint.

1 Pre heat the oven to 220°C, season the beef
well with salt and pepper and drizzle with a
little olive oil.

2 Roast for 50 minutes for a medium rare
roast and a further 10 minutes for medium,
I personally do not like to cook it any less for
a roast.

3 Resting a roasted joint is as important as
the cooking and a joint of this size will happily
sit for an hour while you get on with all the
other jobs.

4 Place the joint of beef onto a warm clean
tray, pour the fat/dripping into a jug and pour
the glass of red wine into the tray that the beef
was cooked in, scrape up all the bits that were
stuck to the tray (in chef terms this is called
deglazing) boil for a few minutes add the
glacé and about 200ml of water and any
scrapes of meat that you roasted alongside
the beef, simmer very gently.

Yorkshire puddings

5 To cook the Yorkshire puddings, pour a little
of the dripping into a muffin tray with 12 cups
and place into a hot oven at about 220°C for
10 minutes, then carefully remove the tray
and pour in the batter and fill up each cup two
thirds; place straight back into the oven and
cook at 220°C for 10 minutes and a further 10
minutes at 180°C. They should be golden, well
risen and slightly crisp. Remove from the tray
and keep warm.

6 Pick the watercress into small bunches
removing most of the stalk.

7 Take the beef off the bone and catch any juice
that comes out, keep the bone for stock, let the
beef rest for a few more minutes while you dish
up your vegetables. Generously slice the beef
and serve two slices onto each warm plate.
Pour any juice into the gravy, strain into a clean
saucepan and pour over the plated meat and
serve with a small bunch of watercress and a
Yorkshire pudding.

8 Serve with roast potatoes and seasonal
vegetables and offer a pot of mustard and
horseradish cream. That's what Sundays are
all about.

Trifle

This light and elegant trifle is far removed from the type my Gran would serve us made with packet sponge, Rowntree's jelly, Bird's custard, dream topping, and finished with hundreds and thousands. How times have changed – though I loved it back then with Gran.

I loved it back then with Gran

Rhubarb and Champagne trifle

Ingredients

200g rhubarb
100g sugar
200ml Champagne
1 tablespoon of lemon juice
1 tablespoon of orange juice
3 leaves of gelatine
3 egg yolks
50g sugar
25g flour
250ml milk
1 vanilla pod
300ml double cream
100g flaked almonds

Serves 4

1 Dissolve 100g of sugar in the Champagne with the orange juice and lemon juice, bring to a simmer and add the rhubarb cut into bite size pieces, poach until just soft, lift out the rhubarb, strain the juice (you should have about 400ml) while still warm add the gelatine which has been soaked in cold water.

2 Place the rhubarb into the bottom of six glass dishes and pour the jelly on top; leave to set.

3 Make the custard; heat the milk with the vanilla pod split in two. In a bowl mix the egg yolks with 50g sugar, add the flour and mix well. Add the milk and stir well, pour back into the pan and cook over a slow heat until thick. Pour through a sieve into a clean bowl and leave to cool.

4 When cool add 100ml of cream and pour on top of the jelly, whip the rest of the cream and spoon on top. Serve with the almond sprinkled on top.

To begin with

Starters at Hilaire always tended to be on the slightly large size. Perhaps it was something to do with my appetite, or where I come from in the valleys of Wales.

Starters at Hilaire always tended to be on the slightly large size. Perhaps it was something to do with my appetite, or where I come from in the valleys of Wales, although as a little boy I do not recall my mum serving a starter at home. If Susan, or more than likely my longstanding second chef, Den, ever made a point about the size of the portions my reply would be that it was a Taffy portion!

I was also finding that when Susan and I ate out at other restaurants she would more often than not be able to finish a starter and a main course. Added to this, starters would usually read much more interestingly than mains. After all, mains are normally a large slab of meat or fish with veggies and a sauce.

Susan then began to order just two starters and managed to finish them, which gave me the idea to split up our menu. I did not want to offer an individually priced menu but I thought that offering two starters at a set price would be a good alternative to the starter and main. It wasn't totally original, as Antony Worrall Thompson back in the 80s ran a restaurant serving starters and puds but no main course.

The following collection of starters can be offered as a light supper or served before the main event.

Asparagus

When we start getting deliveries of wonderful new season English asparagus in May it really excites me. The season is very short and it will all be over by the first week in June, which is why at that time it's all over the menu; in salads to go with grilled turbot or topped with fried fresh morel mushrooms and a poached egg; in soups or, the most simple of all, with a balsamic dressing and Parmesan.

Simple things in cooking are the hardest, and because there is no room for error the asparagus has to be very fresh, which is why asparagus from California, Mexico or Peru is nowhere near as good. Boil them in salted water, don't over or undercook them, add a tasty dressing and you have perfection on a plate.

Some people say you should not peel asparagus, but that's a matter of taste. I do, as I think it looks better and the customer is paying for me to do it. But be careful when peeling these glorious spears; use a sharp peeler, do not press too hard and keep turning the spear as you peel. Once peeled, they are best cooked straight away. If that's not possible, cover them with a wet, cold tea towel until needed.

Asparagus soup

Ingredients

110g butter

1 large onion, peeled and chopped

500g asparagus cut into 2.5cm pieces and the hard stalk removed (if you come across ones called sprue which are thin and straggly and much cheaper then this can be used)

1 litre water

300ml cream

A few sprigs of tarragon (optional)

Salt and pepper

Serves 4

1 Melt the butter and gently cook the onions until soft.

2 Add the asparagus, season with salt and pepper, cover with a lid and gently cook until they start to break down.

3 When soft add the water to just cover them and simmer for 5 minutes.

4 Purée in a blender adding the tarragon if you wish, then pass through a sieve, one that's not too fine. Check the seasoning and add the cream.

Asparagus with balsamic vinegar
and shaved Parmesan

Ingredients

6 to 8 asparagus spears per person

2 finely chopped shallots

4 tablespoons of the very best aged
balsamic vinegar you can buy

A wedge of Parmesan preferably
Parmigiano Reggiano

150ml extra virgin olive oil

Salt and pepper

Serves 4

1 Have ready a pot of well salted boiling water.

2 Put the shallots and vinegar in a bowl and
add the olive oil in a fine stream. Season
with salt and pepper.

3 Boil the asparagus for four to five minutes,
lift out with a pair of tongs onto a tray so you
can arrange them in a line, and then place the
on four warm plates.

4 Spoon some of the dressing over and with a
potato peeler cut thin strips of Parmesan and
throw on top of each plate and serve at once.

5 The dressing will keep for at least two weeks.
Try it with some grilled fish and the left over
Parmesan is a good store cupboard ingredient
and good for grating into your risottos.

Peppers

Peppers are essentially a summer vegetable, but these days in our shops we see them all the year round having being forcefully grown in Holland. Real peppers, which you will see in the market stalls on the continent, are all shapes and sizes; some with slightly green patches. All peppers will go red when fully ripe: a green pepper is an under-ripe pepper grown to suit the supermarket's ideas of shape and size, and has no taste which is why it can be rather bitter. Peppers can be divided into two main groups; the sweet pepper and the chilli pepper. In general, sweet peppers are large, with thick, mild-flavoured flesh, while chilli peppers are smaller and conical in shape and with much more fire in their taste.

Peppers make great salads to go with summery barbecue food. For simple, roasted peppers cut into strips and dress with olive oil,

salt, pepper and basil, add a dash of red wine vinegar and maybe some grated boiled eggs to build on your salad.

Red peppers are also used to make Gazpacho, the famous cold Spanish soup. Stuffed peppers have been around for decades but the most classic and copied is the Piedmontese pepper. The original recipe comes from Elizabeth David's *Italian Food*, published in 1954. It was then adapted by Franco Taruschio at the Walnut Tree Inn where I discovered it and have copied it ever since.

At Tyddyn Llan the peppers are served with buffalo mozzarella which comes from the Campania area of Italy, around Naples, and is flown over weekly. If you use mozzarella, try to buy it from a cheese shop rather than in plastic bags as it's all down to the taste.

Piedmontese peppers

Ingredients

4 red peppers
Salt and pepper
4 garlic cloves peeled
8 ripe vine or plum tomatoes, skinned
100ml olive oil
16 tinned anchovy fillet drained

Serves 4

1 Preheat the oven to 220°C.

2 Cut the peppers in half lengthways and remove the cores and seeds. Season the insides with salt and pepper.

3 Slice the garlic very thinly and distribute between the peppers.

4 Place a tomato inside each pepper, and season again.

5 Place in a roasting tray and pour the olive oil over each pepper, cover with foil and bake in the oven for 45 minutes.

6 Leave to cool, and then place the anchovy fillets in a criss-cross pattern on each pepper. Serve at room temperature.

Gazpacho

Ingredients

500ml water
1 red pepper
1 green pepper
2 teaspoons of salt
1 teaspoon of pepper
1 cucumber
375ml olive oil
3 cloves garlic
5 whole shallots
8 ripe plum tomatoes
Large tablespoon of tomato ketchup
20 leaves of mint
Dash of Tabasco
2 bread rolls
100ml red wine vinegar
500g of ice

Serves 8

1 Cut all the vegetables into a dice, break the bread into small pieces and add all the other ingredients except the ice.

2 Leave to marinate for 6 hours.

3 Purée and pass through a sieve, add the ice and leave to chill, preferably overnight.

Soups

As a young chef many years ago, making soups did not interest me. It was boring. I wanted to do the fancy stuff. But then one day it hit me: soup may be simple, but it takes a good cook to make a tasty soup, and from that day I have always been the one to make the soup at the restaurant.

There are so many varieties and every country or region has their speciality: Cawl from Wales, Scotch broth from Scotland, Minestrone from Italy and the French give us the Onion Soup. Soups are personal and it is what you have at hand, or your preference, that determines how your soup will turn out.

There are a few basic rules to follow when making soups: if it's a green soup such as watercress you must add the green vegetables to boiling liquid to preserve its colour; for other puréed soups – leek and potato or carrot – you must cook the vegetables until they are very soft and have released their flavours before adding the stock. I believe the same applies to chunky soups that are not to be puréed as well. Butternut squash works just as well as

pumpkin, also this is the only time I would ever suggest using a chicken or vegetable stock cube – though it has to be Knorr – in place of homemade stock.

Pumpkin soup

Ingredients

1 kg of pumpkin (use iron bar variety
    if you can, otherwise use butternut squash)
1 large onion peeled and chopped
150g butter, unsalted
Salt and pepper
1½ litres of chicken stock or water

Serves 9

1 Melt the butter and add the onion, cook until very soft, add the pumpkin with salt and pepper, cover with a lid and let it all break down slowly over a low heat.

2 When the pumpkin is very soft (quite a lot of liquid will have come out) cover with stock or water and simmer for 10 minutes.

3 Purée the soup in a blender and pass through a sieve into a clean saucepan, check for seasoning and serve.

Leek and bacon soup

Ingredients

4 large leeks, cleaned
200g of pancetta or dry cured bacon
100g unsalted butter
1 litre chicken stock
Small French bread stick
100g of Cheddar, Double Gloucester
   or Parmesan
Salt and pepper

Serves 4

1 Cut the leeks into very small dice and cut the bacon into small strips.

2 Melt the butter and add the bacon and leeks to the pan, cook very slowly until the leeks are soft, add chicken stock, leave to simmer for about 10 minutes and season with salt and pepper. Cut the bread into thin slices and place on a tray, bake in an oven or under the grill until golden brown.

3 Grate the cheese.

4 When you are ready to serve, heat the grill, ladle the soup into oven proof bowls, top with three or four croutons and then with the grated cheese. Place under the grill until the cheese is melted and has a nice colour. This soup is a Welsh take on the classic French onion soup.

Curried pea and lettuce soup

Ingredients

1 onion chopped
1 iceberg lettuce
350g peas, fresh or frozen
50g butter
25g flour
1 tablespoon curry powder
1¼ litres of chicken stock

Serves 6

1 Sweat the chopped onion in butter until soft then add the sliced lettuce until broken down.

2 Add the curry powder and flour and cook through.

3 Add the chicken stock and simmer for 5 minutes.

4 Add the peas and simmer until they are cooked.

5 Purée and pass through a sieve.

Cawl

During the very cold winter days a good hot soup warms us up. In Wales the traditional broth is called Cawl. It was the 'All in one stew' and was at one time the staple diet of many Welsh families. The meat from the pot was served for one meal with the broth being kept overnight for the next day. Many of the older generation remember it with affection and a few of the younger generation still make it. With our modern healthy eating habits the recipe for Cawl has seen changes over the years – the meat is leaner, the vegetables more abundant and both are served well skimmed of fat.

Ways of making Cawl vary from region to region in Wales. In most cases it simply consisted of what was to hand. I have read recipes for Cawl using bacon and brisket of beef but coming from the south I have always used lamb. It would be good if Prince Charles called for mutton to be used more - to make the Cawl with mutton.

Another excellent soup for cold winter days is split pea, ham and vegetable. This is one of my mum's favourites. Just boil a ham hock in a large pot of water for one hour, skimming the top as scum forms, then add a 200g packet of dried split peas and cook for 20 minutes. Finally add diced root vegetables such as swede, parsnips, celeriac and carrots. Once they are cooked add some chopped leeks and cook for a further 10 minutes. This is just a rough guide but use as little or as much of a selection of vegetables as you wish. When making these types of soups it is always better in large amounts and the beauty of them is whatever is left over freezes well.

Cawl

Ingredients

1 kg of shoulder of lamb
2 onions
4 large carrots
1 swede
2 parsnips
2 leeks
1 small celeriac or 3 celery sticks
A few sprigs of thyme and parsley
2 large potatoes, peeled (optional)

Serves 10

1 Bone out the shoulder of lamb or ask the butcher to do it for you but keep the bones and ask for some extra.

2 Cut the meat into small dice, removing any large pieces of fat and any sinew.

3 Peel the root vegetables and cut into small dice the same size as the meat, clean the leeks and chop and also chop the onion.

4 In a large saucepan heat a little oil and fry the meat until brown. Remove the meat from the pan onto a tray or plate, then fry the onion for a few minutes but do not colour.

5 Put the meat back in the pan with all the vegetables except the leeks, mix well, cover with cold water and add the lamb bones. Bring to the boil, skim and add the parsley and thyme, simmer for about 1 hour adding more water if needed. Add the leeks and simmer until tender.

6 Remove the bones and herbs, check the seasoning and serve. If using the potatoes add after 30 minutes of cooking.

Fish soup

Whenever I see fish soup on a menu I am always tempted to order it. I just love the flavours. Making it is pretty satisfying also, especially when you see what goes into it. Most people tend to think of 'soupe de poissons' as Mediterranean, and something you would eat on the sunny terrace of a seaside café rather than huddled indoors around a warm fire.

Go anywhere in France where they have fresh fish, and you will find that reddy-brown thick broth and its accompaniment of Rouille and croutons, which are a classic and a must to go with the soup. I also like some grated Parmesan to go with it, but I know that some chefs disagree.

Rouille is very simple to make and this recipe comes from Joyce Molyneux when she ran the famous Carved Angel restaurant. Simply liquidize a 200g can of pimientos with one clove of garlic, two small seeded chillies and a few tablespoons of olive oil until smooth.

Rouille and croutons are a must to go with the soup

Fish soup

Ingredients

2kg of mixed fish, scaled and gutted

2 onions, chopped

2 heads of fennel, chopped

2 sticks of celery, chopped

3 carrots, chopped

1 head of garlic, cut into four

4 bay leaves

A large sprig of thyme

1 small orange, quartered

A generous pinch of saffron

1 tablespoon of rice

Half bottle of white wine

Half bottle of red wine

1 x 700g jar of passata

Serves 10

1 Cut the fish into large pieces, heat the largest saucepan you have, add olive oil and fry the fish in small batches.

2 Add the onion, fennel, celery, carrot and garlic and fry until lightly brown, return the fish back to the pan and add the wine. Boil for 5 minutes.

3 Add the herbs, passata, rice and saffron, give it a big stir and let it gently cook for a further 10 minutes.

4 Now add enough cold water to cover the fish and bring to a gentle simmer. Skim the scum that will come to the surface and cook for a further 50 minutes.

5 Break down the soup into a purée in a mouli or blender and then pass through a fine sieve. Pour into a clean saucepan, bring to a boil and skim. Adjust the seasoning and serve with croutons and garnish with fish and prawns if desired, rouille and grated cheese. This soup does freeze well.

Lobster

During the summer months lobsters are at their best as the shells are full and meaty, so make the most of them while you can. I know how difficult it is to buy a live lobster but as with all fish, our coastline of Wales has plenty. When you visit seaside towns like Barmouth and Aberdyfi you always see loads of lobster pots, but it's rare to see anyone selling them on the coast, so ask your local fishmonger and he should be able to supply you with some.

Lobsters live in cold water, and prefer rocky ground, like most crustaceans. As soon as the water warms up they move to shallower, warmer water so if you know where to look when the tide is out you might find a lobster hiding in the many holes and ledges.

A cock lobster is best used in salads as it has large claws containing succulent meat. A hen lobster is preferable for dishes with sauces as the roe inside gives an exceptional depth to the flavour of the sauce. The tail of the hen is broader than that of the cock, and the top swimmerettes are soft compared to the male's hard bony ones.

To cook a lobster you will need a large pan with a lid and enough boiling water to immerse the lobster completely. The water should be fairly salty with aromatics of carrot, onion, celery, thyme, parsley and bay leaves, boil for 5 minutes. Then holding the lobster firmly over the back, tucking the tail underneath, drop the lobster into the water and put the lid back on. Bring to the boil for 1 minute, switch on the heat and leave for 15 minutes, remove from the pot to cool. If you are going to eat your lobster cold leave to cool in the water. You can store the lobster in the water in a fridge for up to three days.

To prepare a lobster have it on a board with the tail extended and split lengthways using a heavy knife. Discard the stomach sac from the head and the viscera from the tail. Reserve any juice from inside. Do not rinse it under water as many misguided chefs do, as this washes away the flavour. Scrape out all the gungy meat from the head. Disjoint the claws and carefully crack the end joint, removing the meat in the largest pieces possible. Use a small teaspoon or lobster pick to extract meat from all the other joints. Cut the tail into five pieces and place in the opposite shell to where it came from and divide the rest of the meat between the heads. Now pour any juices back over the lobsters. This can be done hours in advance and covered with cling film.

At Tyddyn Llan as a starter I serve a half lobster grilled with a butter of coriander, lime and ginger, this butter is also very good melted over a piece of cooked skate or monkfish.

Grilled Lobster with coriander, lime and ginger butter

Ingredients

675g lobster (approx weight)
250g packet of butter
1 small bunch of coriander
1 small piece of ginger, peeled
1 or 2 red chillis depending on how hot you
    like it
2 cloves of garlic
Juice of 1 lime
Salt and pepper

Serves 2

1 Have the butter at room temperature in a bowl, grate the ginger and garlic and mix into the butter with the lime juice.

2 Deseed the chilli and finely chop; add to the butter.

3 Roughly chop the coriander leaves and stalks; add to the butter.

4 Mix well and season with salt and pepper.

5 Lay two sheets of cling film on top of each other on a table.

6 Scrape the butter out of the bowl and place on the cling film. Roll up tightly into a large cylinder shape. This will keep in a fridge for up to a week.

7 Pre-heat an oven to 200°C and a grill on the highest setting.

8 Have the lobster prepared and on a tray, slice the butter and place onto the lobster.

9 Place the lobster in the oven for 5 minutes then under the hot grill until golden brown. Serve straight away.

Aubergine

The aubergine is probably my wife Susan's favourite vegetable, and I am constantly telling her off for having a spoon in the Imam Bayildi. She even bought cushions for our house with aubergines on and Gordon Ramsay gave her a plate with an aubergine painted on it which now hangs on the wall in the bar at Tyddyn Llan.

There are hundreds of ways in which to prepare them. Their flavour is subtle and to a certain extent fugitive, so it's important to combine aubergines with strong flavours. They are an ideal match for pungent herbs, spices and Welsh lamb.

There are many interesting ways to prepare aubergines and they lend themselves to many cooking methods: grilling, roasting, stewing and frying, but be careful when frying as they can act as a sponge for oil and can end up tasting heavy. A great way to cook them is on a griddled plate and keep turning them until they go very soft. This gives them a smoky taste. Peel them once they are cold and use them in salads or as aubergine purée.

Aubergine is the French name we adopted. We used to call it eggplant as the Americans still do because it looks like a perfectly shaped goose egg. I always think of Mediterranean food and the aubergine. It is surprising to learn that its original home is from tropical Asia.

Imam Bayildi

Ingredients

4 medium aubergines, cut into large cubes
2 onions
3 cloves of garlic
1 teaspoon of ground cumin
2 tins of plum tomatoes
½ bunch of flat parsley
2 tablespoons of raisins, golden if possible
Olive oil
Some natural yoghurt
Salt

Serves 6

1 Chop the onion and garlic and cook slowly in olive oil until soft. Add a pinch of salt as this makes the process faster.

2 In a deep fat fryer with good vegetable oil fry the aubergines until golden. Drain into a colander over a bowl.

3 Add the cumin and cook for a few minutes. Strain the tomatoes and break them up. Add to the onions, cook for a further 5 minutes until thick.

4 Add the aubergines and cook for two or three minutes until all the flavours mix together. Add the flat parsley which has been roughly chopped.

5 Serve Turkish style, which is to say lukewarm and in a leisurely fashion with a dollop of natural yoghurt and a little olive oil.

Terrine of calves liver, bacon and foie gras

Ingredients

500g finely diced calves liver

500g sausage meat

400g foie gras

400g diced streaky bacon

5 finely chopped shallots, cooked in butter

2 tablespoons of green peppercorns

½ tablespoon of fresh picked thyme

100ml port

50ml brandy

Italian back fat or streaky bacon cut into
  very thin strips

Serves 12

1 Place all the ingredients except the back fat into a very large bowl and mix well.

2 Line three terrine dishes with the Italian fat overlapping the sides.

3 Fill the terrines with the mixture and cover with the fat.

4 Cover with foil and place in a deep roasting tray with warm water.

5 Cook at 160°C for 1½ hours or until firm to the touch.

6 Leave to cool for at least one day.

Terrines

I have always enjoyed making terrines and pâtés, and the great pleasure you get when you turn the terrine out and cut the first slice. I learnt how to make terrines more out of trial and error and I will never forget my first attempt at terrine foie gras and my horror when I lifted the lid to see this pool of melted fat. While parfait of foie gras and chicken liver are wonderful and smooth, nothing beats a good chunky pâté. This recipe is one of Susan's favourites which is rather surprising as she is not a lover of calves liver.

Confit

Confit is a piece of pork, duck or goose, cooked in its own fat and stored in a pot to preserve it. It's one of the oldest forms of preserving food and is a speciality of the Basque region in the south west of France. Before deep freezers I remember my mother doing something similar to her precious runner beans in the summer, so she could eat them at Christmas.

The long life of confit and the fact that it can be eaten hot or cold, together with its delicate flavours, have made it one of the high dishes of French gastronomy. It is used in the preparation of garbue, a hearty soup, cassoulet (a wonderful dish of pork, sausage and white beans) and duck or goose confit in a rich tomato sauce. It's also great warm in salads or with lentils and anchoïade, which is an olive oil, basil and anchovy paste.

Anchoïade

Ingredients

300g anchovies

500ml extra virgin olive oil

6 cloves garlic

2 teaspoons finely chopped thyme

5 tablespoons of chopped basil

3 tablespoons Dijon mustard

3 tablespoons red wine vinegar

1 teaspoon ground pepper

1 Put all ingredients into a food processor and purée whilst slowly adding the olive oil.

2 Store covered in the fridge until required.

salad of duck confit and butter beans

Ingredients

4 duck legs
2 bulbs of garlic
8 bay leaves
A small bunch of thyme
4 tablespoons of sea salt
2 tablespoons of cracked peppercorns
900g tin of goose fat or lard
4 tablespoons of Anchoïade
4 tablespoons of vinaigrette
Italian flat parsley
A French baguette, cut into 20 thin slices
250g butter beans*

Serves 4

*If you can get the Spanish Judión del Barco beans it will make a difference. Soak them over night in cold water. The next day drain the beans and place into a clean saucepan, cover with water, add two bay leaves and a stick of celery, bring to a simmer and cook slowly for about 1 ½ hours until tender. Top up the water if necessary or you can put them into a moderate oven with a lid on if you wish, but do check the water level. Once cooked add a good splash of olive oil, season with salt and freshly ground pepper and leave in their juice until required.

To cook the confit

1 In a large bowl sprinkle some of the sea salt, a few bay leaves, thyme and peppercorns. Lay the duck legs on top and add the rest of the ingredients except the fat. Cover with cling film and leave for 24 hours.

2 The next day wash the salt off the legs and pat dry and in a large oven proof saucepan melt the goose fat and add the duck legs and all the other ingredients and bring to a gentle simmer. Cover with a lid.

3 Put in the oven, preheated to 130°C, and cook for 1½ hours by which time the fat should be clear and the legs showing a lot of bone – as the 'meats rides up on a mini skirt on a white thigh' as Alastair Little puts it.

4 Leave to cool then place in a small bucket or jar covered with the strained fat. Leave for at least a week.

5 To reheat the confit take the duck out of the fat and place on a tray and heat through in a hot oven until the skin is brown and crisp.

To assemble the dish

1 Lay the slices of bread on a tray, drizzle with olive oil and bake in an oven at 180°C until golden brown.

2 Heat the duck confit in the oven, leave to cool slightly, remove the shin and break up the meat and put into a large bowl. Warm the butter beans and roughly chop the parsley.

3 Add the butter beans and parsley to the duck and season with the vinaigrette.

4 Spread the anchoïade onto the croutons, divide the duck and bean salad onto four warm plates and arrange three to five croutons around. Drizzle with a little extra olive oil and serve. Lentils also work very well instead of the butter beans.

salad of fennel, artichokes,
sun-dried tomatoes and shaved Parmesan

This salad blew me away the first time I ever tried it at the Walnut Tree Inn. It was a new dish on the menu and they served with a flatbread called Crescente.

When I got back to the kitchen at Hilaire I always tried to fry the artichoke to make it crisp but nothing matched Franco's version. So, with a lot of courage, on probably my fourth visit, and after ordering this salad each time to try and suss it out, I asked Franco how he got the artichokes so crisp. 'Use these,' he said, pointing to cases of Italian cooked and marinated artichokes. 'Just thinly slice and fry in a hot deep fat fryer'. Problem sorted.

Ingredients

8 marinated artichokes

8 sun-dried tomatoes in oil, thinly sliced

1 bulb of fennel, thinly sliced on a mandoline
   with the core removed

A chunk of Parmesan to shave as much
   as you wish onto the top

A handful of good salad leaves per person

Serves 4

1 Put the fennel, sun-dried tomatoes and salad into a large bowl.

2 Deep fry the artichokes until crisp, add to the salad, mix well and pile onto four large plates.

3 Top with shavings of the finest Parmesan.

smoked eel, bacon and new potato salad

This is such a simple dish with just three elements and a good dressing and, to my mind, it makes a great start to a meal. When we were in London our eels were supplied by a great character called Derek Beales. His company was called Beales Eels. It was a great product and he supplied me for more than 12 years until we left. Sadly, when we opened up in Wales we were no longer able to get his wonderful smoked eel and now he is no longer with us. But you can buy eels via the post as we do from Brown and Forrest which I think are as good as Derek's.

Ingredients

150g of diced good quality pancetta or dry cured streaky bacon

300g smoked eel fillet

400g of cooked and peeled new potatoes such as Ratte, Jersey or Pembroke

Vinaigrette

Chopped chives

A few sprigs of chervil if you wanted to be chefy and poncy about things.

Serves 4

1 In a frying pan with a little sunflower oil gently cook the bacon until very crisp. Keep warm.

2 Slice, or half if small, the potatoes and reheat in a basket within a pot of hot water or in the microwave.

3 Slice the eel into thin strips.

4 Put the potatoes into a bowl and dress with a little vinaigrette and chives.

5 Pile onto the centre of four warm plates, top with the smoked eel and the bacon, add a little of the bacon fat to the bowl the potatoes were dressed in and a dash more of the vinaigrette and drizzle around the salad. Top with a few sprigs of chervil.

Smoked salmon

Smoked Salmon has always been classed as a luxury food, and even these days with farmed salmon the price of four slices from a supermarket at £3.99 is still out of reach for most pockets. But it is well worth it for that special occasion. How better to begin your Sunday off than with a few slices of smoked salmon with lightly scrambled free range eggs and, if it's more of a brunch, a glass of Bucks Fizz!

There are many styles of smoked salmon, so to find the smoked salmon that you like you should try different varieties because they do vary enormously as regional specialities find their way into the shops. Some are pale and oak-smoked, while others are over-salted and artificially dyed. My preference would be for a wild fish oak-smoked, but a wild fish these days can cost £20 or more a kilo and that's before the smoking process. I must admit, though, that in the past when I have had wild salmon smoked for me it was not always the most successful as wild fish do vary enormously in fat content. So these days I buy a Bradan Orach fish from Loch Fyne, which is marinated in sea salt and smoked for 24 hours. Loch Fyne sell direct via the internet if you fancy trying their salmon.

There are two smoking methods, hot and cold. The former is a little like cooking in a smokey oven at a low temperature, but cold smoking takes longer and requires all sorts of skill to get the product right. The ideal way to smoke a salmon would be to take a fresh salmon, split and fillet it, dry cure with sea salt and brown sugar, then get a whisky barrel, chip it, burn it, and smoke your salmon for eight hours. Alternatively find a trustworthy supplier who will do all this for you.

smoked salmon terrine
with horseradish cream

Ingredients

20 slices of smoked salmon
500g of hot smoked salmon
250g cream cheese
200ml double cream
Juice of half a lemon
Salt and a pinch of cayenne pepper
1 tablespoon of fresh chopped dill or chervil

Serves 8

You can halve the recipe and use individual moulds.

1 Line a small terrine with cling film. It's best to rub some vegetable oil on the inside of the terrine or moulds first.

2 Line the moulds or terrine with the sliced smoked salmon overlapping the sides, keeping any trimmings.

3 Flake the hot smoked salmon and put into a food processor with the trimmings, cream cheese and lemon juice. Purée to a smooth paste.

4 Add the double cream, and a pinch of cayenne pepper. Whiz a little more but be very careful not to overwork the mix at this point.

5 Check the seasoning as it may need a touch of salt. Fold in the chopped herbs.

6 Scrape out of the bowl, fill the terrine and cover with the overlapping slices. Chill for at least 6 hours.

7 Serve with cucumber salad, horseradish cream and hot toast.

Horseradish cream

Ingredients

300ml double cream
1 tablespoon of freshly grated horseradish
1 tablespoon of horseradish relish
1 teaspoon of Dijon mustard
1 tablespoon of lemon juice
Salt and pepper

1 Put all the ingredients in a bowl and whisk until slightly thick, keep in the fridge until needed. This is also great with the Sunday roast beef.

Broad beans

From the beginning of Spring your local vegetable dealers will have an abundance of fresh broad beans and peas, the most summery vegetables I can think of. I just love their different flavours, but they can be something of a problem. Once picked, you must use them as quickly as possible as they deteriorate rapidly and the ones you see in the shops are going to be at least three days old already. This is why most growers in this country sell their crops to Captain Birdseye and his mates, who claim that every pea and bean harvested at dawn is picked, hulled, graded, blanched and frozen within four hours; some achievement.

Broad beans and peas have been bobbing about in our cooking pots for centuries. We started growing peas in the 17th century and you can go as far back as the Bronze Age for the broad bean. In those days the ones that were not eaten were dried for later use. In the Middle Eastern countries, dried broad beans are still very much a delicacy today.

Once your fresh broad beans and peas are in the kitchen, you'll need endless patience for the podding, but the end product is well worth the effort. The only difference in cooking the peas to the broad beans is that while lightly salted water with a sprig of mint is ideal for peas, broad beans are best boiled in unsalted water, as salt will only toughen the skins (you can season them before serving). Once the broad beans grow large the skins will become hard and so even more patience is required to peel the skin away, which results in a bright green bean which looks as good as it tastes.

Before the asparagus season finishes, try a salad of peas, broad beans and asparagus dressed with mint and extra virgin olive oil, topped with Parmesan shavings. A true taste of summer.

A true taste of summer.

Tagliatelle with broad beans,
bacon and mustard

Ingredients

200g tagliatelle, homemade or fresh from
   the supermarket
200g blanched and skinned broad beans
150g streaky dry cured Welsh bacon with the
   rind removed
1 small onion, finely chopped
75g unsalted butter
200ml double cream
2 tablespoons of Dijon mustard
Salt

Serves 4

1 Melt the butter in a saucepan. Add the onion
and cook until soft, cut the bacon into small
cubes and add to the onion. Cook for a further
5 minutes.

2 Add the cream, the broad beans and the
mustard and heat through.

3 Cook the pasta in a generous amount of
boiling salted water, and then drain thoroughly.
Add to the sauce and serve.

4 Portioning pasta can cause a messy problem
and some people might get more beans than
the next person. So if you have four small
saucepans divide the sauce between them.
Reheat the pasta in single portions in a pot of
water using a sieve add to the sauce then serve
straight onto a plate. No mess but three extra
pans to wash up.

signature dishes

Every chef has a signature dish, one that they are proud of and can cook blindfolded. It's the dish that you have in your mind as you drive to the restaurant and are disappointed if it's not on the menu. I cannot remember going to the Walnut Tree and not ordering a plate of Franco's wonderful Bresoala, or the chicken and goats cheese mousse when Rowley Leigh was cooking at Kensington Place. Shaun Hill is still cooking his famous sweetbreads with potato and olive cake after 18 years and I always order it, similarly with Gordon Ramsay's ravioli of lobster and Richard Corrigan's crubeens.

This is a collection of my dishes that I have been cooking for many years; most of them are always on my menu if the ingredients are available and in season and when there is room to squeeze them onto the menu. They are plates of food that not only do I enjoy cooking immensely, I also love eating them too and whenever friends come around for supper you can bet I will proudly serve one or two of these dishes.

Every chef has a signature dish, one that they are proud of and can cook blindfolded.

Left: Preparing roast saddle of local lamb.

Red mullet

It still amazes me that the British will eat fish on the bone when on holidays in France, Italy or Spain but if I was to be brave enough to serve fish on the bone at the restaurant there would be uproar – with maybe the exception of Dover Sole.

Red mullet is one fish that should really always be cooked whole, even with the innards still in. Okay, maybe you should just leave the liver in, as it's known as the woodcock of the sea.

At Tyddyn Llan we serve a fillet of lightly grilled red mullet over a spiced purée of aubergine and dressed with a chilli and garlic oil. Then with the bones we make a splendid fish soup to serve on Sunday lunch which makes for good housekeeping.

If you cannot get red mullet, try grey mullet but only if it's very fresh, with its eyes really bright, though I have eaten good farmed sea bream, so you could try that too.

Grilled red mullet with chilli and garlic oil

Ingredients

4 large red mullet about 500g each filleted
Olive oil
Sea salt (Halen Môn is very good)

Serves 4

1 Heat the grill to the maximum.

2 Season the fillets of fish with salt and pepper and place on a tray lightly oiled with olive oil. Place the fish onto the tray with the skin facing up.

3 Put the fillet under the grill and cook until just done.

4 Heat the aubergine purée, and place a spoon ful into four heated bowls. Mix a little chopped parley into the dressing and pour a small amount around the purée.

5 Place the cooked fish on top of the purée and serve.

chilli and garlic oil

Ingredients

3 cloves of chopped garlic
2 anchovy fillets
½ tablespoon of chilli flakes
2 tablespoons of sunflower oil
75ml of extra virgin olive oil
Chopped parsley

1 Heat the garlic, anchovy and chilli flakes in the sunflower oil until the anchovy melts. Remove from the heat.

2 Add the olive oil and leave to cool.

Aubergine purée

Ingredients

3 aubergines
2 cloves of garlic
Juice of ¼ lemon
½ teaspoons of ground cumin
1 tablespoon of tahini
125ml extra virgin olive oil
Salt and pepper

1 First grill the aubergines on a solid top or bake in a hot oven until soft. When cool peel and leave to drain in a colander over a bowl with a plate and a weight on top for 1 hour.

2 Place all the ingredients in a food processor and purée, slowly adding the olive oil. Season to taste.

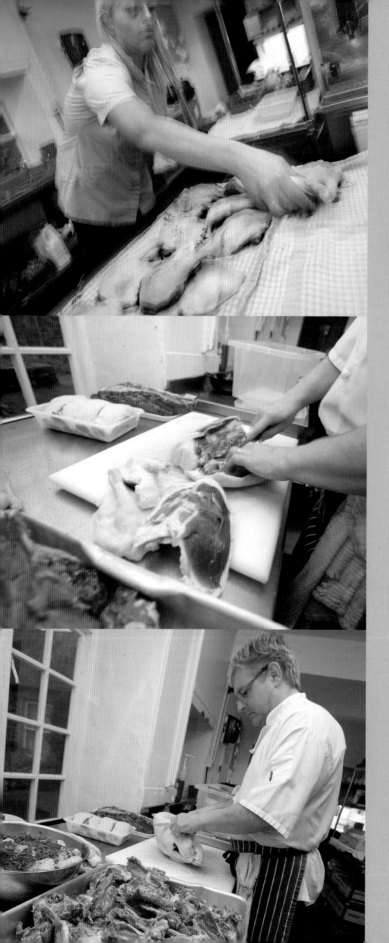

Duck

Roast duck and apple sauce has been a favourite of mine for many years. I still remember duck in my days at the Drangway restaurant in Swansea when we would roast whole ducks until they were well done and the skin a golden crisp, to be carved at the table by the head waiter, Paco.

It was always a popular dish, and now being back in Wales we are often asked for well done breast of duck, which of course does not work. To achieve a crisp well done duck you have to roast the whole bird. We only have to look at the Chinese who mastered the art centuries ago. Buy whole ducks for this dish, as the carcass is used for the sauce and the legs and fat can be used to make confit. If you like well done, crisp duck confit is ideal.

Breast of Gressingham duck,

potato pancake, cider and apple sauce

Ingredients

4 large Gressingham ducks
2 Granny Smith apples
25g butter
4 large peeled and sliced shallots
6 sticks of celery, chopped
1 large carrot, chopped
1 litre bottle of dry cider
500ml apple juice
Sprig of thyme
4 bay leaves
500ml chicken stock
500ml veal stock
25ml Calvados
Potato pancake mix (see page 194)
Spinach

Serves 8

1 Bone out the ducks and trim the breasts, reserve the fat and legs.

2 Chop the bones and roast in a hot oven until golden brown.

3 Peel and cut the apples into a small dice, melt the butter and cook the apple dice for a few minutes. Add the Calvados and leave to one side. Keep all the trimming, peelings and core.

4 Drain the fat from the roasted bones into a large saucepan and add the shallots, carrots and celery. Cook until slightly brown, drain off any remaining fat. Add the bones back to the pan and pour in the cider and apple juice, bring to the boil, add the thyme, bay leaves and apple trimmings, boil for 5 minutes. Add the chicken and veal stocks and cover with cold water, bring to a gentle simmer. Skim off any fat and scum and simmer for 1 hour.

5 Drain though a fine sieve into a clean saucepan and reduce to a slightly thick sauce.

6 Everything for this dish can be done in advance up to this stage.

7 Season the duck breasts and place two into a large frying pan skin side down and cook until golden. Turn over for 1 minute, then transfer to a tray, drain off the fat and repeat with the other two breasts.

8 Roast in a hot oven 220°C for 10 minutes (for pink) and leave to rest in a warm place for a further 10 minutes while you cook the pancakes and spinach.

9 To serve place a pancake onto four heated plates and top with a spoonful of spinach. Carve the breasts and arrange on top. Spoon the heated sauce over and serve at once.

Laverbread and bass

Bass and laverbread has been a favourite of mine since my early days of cooking at the Drangway. Back in the early 80s, when we would go though lots of bass caught just off the coast, they would all be line-caught and so stiff as a board. We would have to leave them a day just to be able to fillet them. Also they cost no more than 90p a pound (that's showing my age!).

Bass is the one thing Wales has in common with the south of France. We have the best bass swimming around our shores and these days farmed bass is readily available for the home cook and restaurants that choose to serve a one portion fish. The wild type is always my first choice but I run a restaurant where you expect only the best. Fresh line-caught bass have a ravishingly beautiful bright silver belly which darkens to a pale blue grey on its sides. It's a great sporting fish and thrives in rough weather.

Laverbread grows on the rocks and beaches of the Gower coast near Swansea. It has a dark and smooth appearance which makes it distinctive. Traditionally it is boiled for hours to render it to a thick purée. It is sold in the markets and fishmongers in South Wales and it's a part of Welsh culture and heritage that is as famous as our lamb.

The combination of fresh wild bass and a light laverbread butter is a simple combination but it is a light dish and speaks volumes about Welsh food.

Roast wild bass with laverbread butter sauce

Ingredients

4 150g pieces of wild bass, skin on and all
    pin bones removed
2 tablespoons of laverbread
2 tablespoons of double cream
300g fresh spinach
50g extra butter
Beurre blanc (see below)

Serves 4

1 In a saucepan add two tablespoons of
laverbread with 2 tablespoons of cream,
bring to the boil and add half the beurre blanc.

2 Season the fish and coat lightly with olive oil.
Place onto a hot griddle skin side down, until
the skin is crisp. Place onto an oiled tray and
bake in a hot oven at 200°C for 5 minutes.

3 While the fish is cooking, in a large pan melt
the extra butter and cook the spinach until
wilted.

4 Serve the bass on a bed of spinach and pour
the laverbread sauce around one side and the
remaining beurre blanc around the other side.

Beurre blanc

Ingredients

4 finely chopped shallots
1 tablespoon of white wine vinegar (I like to
    use the Forum brand)
175ml dry white wine, Muscadet if possible
250g unsalted butter at room temperature
Salt and a pinch of cayenne pepper
Juice of half a lemon

1 Put the white wine, vinegar and shallots into
a saucepan and slowly reduce to a syrup.

2 On a light heat slowly add the butter a little
at a time until it forms a slightly thick sauce.
Season with salt and cayenne pepper. Add the
juice of the half lemon.

3 Strain the sauce into a clean saucepan and
keep warm.

Leg of rabbit

In north Wales we have hundreds of rabbits
running around our fields – normally being
chased by our white cat Bruno. Wild rabbits
do not generally fit in with our menus, but the
farmed rabbits from France always have a
place. I like to bone out the legs and stuff them
with black pudding but if black pudding is not
to your taste some tarragon butter also works
very well.

we use farmed
rabbits from France

Leg of rabbit with black pudding

Ingredients

4 legs of farmed rabbit

200g of sliced Carmarthen ham or
   any good Prosciutto

120g black pudding

50g butter

1 tablespoon chopped tarragon

2 shallots, sliced

150ml white wine

150ml chicken stock

150ml double cream

1 tablespoon Dijon mustard

Serves 4

1 Remove the thigh bones by turning the leg inside out and save the bones. Mix together the 50g of butter and tarragon in small bowl, divide between the cavities of the four legs, cut the black pudding into four and put a piece into each leg. Fold the meat around the pudding to reform the leg.

2 Lay two slices of Carmarthen ham onto a sheet of cling film, place a rabbit leg on top and wrap the ham around the leg. Wrap in the cling film until required. Do the same with the other legs.

3 Chop the saved bones and fry in a little oil with the shallots, add the white wine and reduce by half. Add the chicken stock and boil again until only half is left, add the cream and reduce to a thick silky sauce. Add the mustard and strain though a fine sieve.

4 Pre-heat the oven to 200°C. In a non stick frying pan put a little oil. When hot place the rabbit legs in the pan cook for 1 minute and place into the hot oven for 6 minutes, turn the legs over and continue to roast for another 6 minutes.

5 Take out of the oven and leave to rest in a warm place for 5 to 10 minutes while you get your garnishes ready. Reheat the sauce and pour over the rabbit. Leave the legs whole or carve into two or three slices. A good creamy mash and some spinach goes well with this dish.

Lamb

I have been making this stuffing to go with
saddles of lamb for well over 15 years. It's my
favourite. It's not a dish that is on our à la carte
menu but it's a great one for functions such as
weddings at Tyddyn Llan.

I remember serving this lamb dish at Neville
and Sonia's Ruby Wedding at Hilaire and for
the wedding just outside Banbury of Denise,
who was my great second chef for most of the
90s. These were two great occasions.

The idea for the stuffing came from the great
Australian chef Stephanie Alexander's book,
Feasts and Stories. I always wanted to eat in
her restaurant but unfortunately by the time
we got to visit Australia it had closed down.

Roast saddle of local lamb

with parsley and pine nut stuffing

Ingredients

1 saddle of lamb, with the bone removed,
  but left whole (your butcher will do this
  as it is a very tricky job).
Salt and pepper
2 bunches of fresh flat parsley
6 cloves of garlic, grated
250ml double cream
120g fresh white breadcrumbs
50g pine nuts

Serves 6

1 In a large saucepan of boiling hot water
blanch the parsley for 2 minutes, then plunge
into a bowl of iced water or drain into
a colander and refresh under running cold
water. Drain well and squeeze very dry in a
clean tea towel.

2 Toast the pine nuts until lightly golden.

3 Bring the cream to a boil and add the
grated garlic with the blanched parsley, boil
but be careful that it does not catch on the
bottom of the pan.

4 When the mixture starts to thicken add the
pine nuts and take off the heat. Stir in the
breadcrumbs a little at a time as you may not
need all of them. Stir well and leave to cool.
The stuffing is best made the day before.

5 Lay the saddle on a work bench and carefully
trim as much fat as you can away from the
flank part. Trim the two fillets and season the
meat with salt and pepper.

6 Place the stuffing down the centre, lay the
two fillets on top and roll together, tie tightly
with string and leave until you are ready

7 Preheat the oven to 220°C.

8 Roast the saddle for 25 minutes for pink and
10 more minutes for well done. Leave to rest
for about 20 minutes.

9 Remove the string and cut into fairly thick
slices.

10 Serve with seasonal vegetables, gratin
Dauphinois and a light lamb jus.

when in season
garnish with some
skinned broad beans

Roast pigeon with braised butter
beans and wild mushrooms

Ingredients

4 large squab pigeons

2 shallots, finely chopped

4 bay leaves

4 sprigs of thyme

Salt and pepper

40g butter

300g dry butter beans, soaked overnight and
simmered in water with a bay leaf, a stick
of celery but no salt for about two hours
until soft

150g wild mushrooms, cleaned

2 shallots, roughly chopped

50ml brandy

100ml Madeira

100ml white wine

2 bay leaves, sprig of thyme, parsley stalks

150ml chicken stock

150ml veal or beef stock

Serves 4

1 Remove the pigeons' wish bone and neck
bones and keep to one side.

2 Divide the shallots between the four pigeon
cavities, together with the thyme and bay
leaves, season with salt and pepper and push a
cocktail stick though the legs to secure.

3 Fry the removed bones with the roughly
chopped shallots for a few minutes, add the
brandy, bring to the boil, then add the Madeira
and white wine, reduce by half, add the stocks
and simmer for 30 minutes. Strain and reduce
to a slightly thick sauce.

4 Pre-heat the oven to 220°C, place the
pigeons in a tray, season with salt and pepper
and spread the butter over the breasts. Roast
in the hot oven for 8 minutes, baste with any
juices and butter and turn them over to be
breast down. Cook for a further 4 minutes for a
pink bird, maybe 6 to 8 minutes for well done.

5 Remove from the oven and place on a warm
tray to rest, pour away any fat, deglaze with the
sauce scraping up the goodness left in the tray
and strain back into a clean saucepan.

6 Reheat the butter beans and season with
salt and pepper. Cook the wild mushrooms
in some hot olive oil and season. Remove the
pigeon legs and cook in the oven for a further 4
minutes while you carve the breasts. Arrange
the beans and mushrooms on four heated
plates. Place the breasts on top and finally
the legs. Pour the sauce over. When in season
garnish with some skinned broad beans.

Scallops

This is one of the most popular starters on the menu. I would get lynched by regulars if it was not on the menu. Griddled scallops with vegetable relish and rocket - it's been on my menus for over ten years.

The inspiration for the dish came while eating lunch at the Original Tante Claire on Royal Hospital Road when the chef served raw scallops with a relish and crispy seaweed. From that meal my signature dish was born, and while it may not be completely original you cannot reinvent the wheel.

The secret to the dish is in the ingredients: extra large king scallops, still alive in the shell when they arrive. Scallops are sweet and tender and go well with peppery wild rocket and the sharp zing of the relish.

When in the sea, scallops dance by snapping their shells shut. They push themselves along, moving quickly through the water with graceful leaps and bounds, escaping the enemy and then settling once again on the sea floor. The best scallops are bought alive in the shell, but just how lively they are will depend on how they are fished. The finest scallops of all are caught by divers and are positively mollycoddled compared to the dredged fish one often finds. The problem with dredged ones is they can contain sand and are therefore gritty.

Avoid frozen scallops, and beware if you see pure white scallops as these have often been soaked in water to make them plump, whereas an unsoaked fresh scallop looks slightly off-white. Soaking detracts completely from all that is good about it: taste, texture and cookability.

Griddled scallops with vegetable relish and rocket

Ingredients

8 fresh scallops
100g rocket
50g unsalted butter
1 tablespoon of sunflower oil
2 tablespoon of extra virgin olive oil
1 teaspoon lemon juice
Salt and pepper

For the relish

1 carrot
1 red pepper
2 shallots
1 tablespoon capers
8 small gherkins
8 green olives
1 tablespoon of good red wine vinegar (if you can, buy a bottle of the Forum brand and keep it for special dishes)

Serves 4

1 Peel the carrot and cut into very thin strips, then lay in piles of three and cut into very thin match sticks, then into the smallest dice possible. Repeat with the pepper but don't peel it.

2 Peel and finely chop the shallots.

3 Stone the olives and finely chop with the gherkins and capers.

4 Mix together in a bowl and add the red wine vinegar. This will keep in a fridge for weeks and goes very well with fish cakes.

5 Wash and dry the rocket.

6 When you are ready to serve, melt the butter and keep warm.

7 Put five piles of relish around four plates and heat a non stick frying pan as hot as you dare.

8 Slice the scallops into three and place on a tray, season with salt and pepper and drizzle the sunflower oil over them.

9 Now be brave and add the scallops to the pan, as soon as you have put them all in start turning them and straight away take them out of the pan and onto the plates.

10 Dress the rocket with olive oil and lemon and pile in the centre of the plate then drizzle the melted butter over the scallops.

Sewin

Sewin is the Welsh name for sea trout; it is wild and as near to a salmon as you can get without being one. If salmon is the king of fish, sewin is the Welsh prince. Although sewin is considered to be the same as the brown trout, it migrates to the sea to feed, returning to the river to spawn. It feeds more locally than salmon, hence is more distinctive from region to region.

Distinguishing between salmon and a large sea trout calls for a certain expertise; it is far harder than telling a brown and sea trout apart. To my eyes it's the squarer tail, a longer and blunter mouth which ends past the eye and the number of scales: 12 on a salmon and up to 15 on a sewin, counting from the adipose fin which is the small softer one behind the larger dorsal fin.

Sewin has a paler pink flesh and a more delicate flavour with a high content of essential oils. Fishermen say it is the most exciting fish to catch, particularly at the dead of night and I am sure many would agree it's also one of the most palatable of all fish. Sewin is seasonal, available from May through to August when small 'harvest' 1lb sewin can be plentiful and are delicious for a single portion.

There are many ways to cook sewin, including grilling, frying and poaching. I would advise against being aggressive with the heat and not to over cook the flesh, leaving it slightly pink. If you have a whole fish it would be great to poach it whole and serve it with some herb mayonnaise and salad.

If you don't have a fish kettle big enough you can use a roasting tray, lining it with foil with at least 12 inches of foil overlapping each side. Place the fish in the tray and have ready a hot court bouillon: to water, add a chopped onion, two sliced carrots and celery, a piece of fennel if you have it, together with a few bay leaves and parsley stalks. Simmer for about 20 minutes then add salt and a couple of peppercorns, and now it's ready to poach any fish. Pour the bouillon over the fish and wrap the foil around, simmer on a low heat for 10 minutes then gently turn the fish over, using the foil to do so, simmer for another eight minutes and leave to cool in the liquid. Do this a day in advance or in the morning and you will have feast to impress anyone. Anything that's left over will make fabulous fish cakes. I hope you will be able to buy sewin and see for yourselves what a wonderful fish we have in our Welsh rivers.

sea trout

Grilled sewin with asparagus salad

Ingredients

4 x 200g pieces of sewin with all pin bones
   removed. Leave the scaled skin on, as when
   it's cooked it's crispy and tastes delicious.
200g Pembroke new potatoes, scraped
   and cooked
6 vine tomatoes, blanched, skins and seeds
   removed, then cut into strips
100g French beans cooked
24 asparagus spears
1 shallot, peeled and thinly sliced
200g mix of beurre blanc (see page 77)
Vinaigrette
Salt

1 Have ready the beurre blanc, a pot of salted boiling water, and a large bowl with the tomatoes, shallots and French beans.

2 Heat a non stick pan or a cast iron griddle.

3 Cook the asparagus in the boiling water, and cook the sewin either on the griddle or in the pan with olive oil until just pink.

4 Once the asparagus is cooked remove from water, reheat the new potatoes.

5 Add the asparagus and potatoes to the tomatoes, shallots and beans, dress with vinaigrette and divide onto four heated plates.

6 Place the sewin on top and spoon some beurre blanc over the top.

Shin of veal

Veal was one of the very first restaurant dishes that I ever ordered, the dish in question being Escalope Holstein, a tender slice of veal with a crisp breaded coating and draped with a fried egg (a garnish that perhaps stirred me to my choice).

There is no doubt that the Italians cook the finest veal dishes anywhere in the world. It is their number one meat, whether they fry, grill, braise or roast it, all of which they do very well. Wet roasting is very popular in Italy and involves sealing, seasoning and colouring the meat in hot oil, cooking it half way in the oven, then adding some white wine, a scrap of garlic, some chopped tomato, a sprinkling of herbs and maybe a squeeze of lemon juice. Then it goes back in the oven, is left to rest and the final result is gravy at its best which it makes itself.

My favourite cut of veal by far is the shin. It's a magnificent joint. The great thing about it is that it is tender enough to roast as well as being gently braised or cut into thick slices for *Osso bucco*. Saffron Risotto goes very well with a chunk of braised veal shin.

Osso bucco with saffron rice

Ingredients

75g butter

3 tablespoons olive oil

Salt and pepper

4 pieces of shin of veal

Flour

175ml white wine

250ml chicken stock (optional)

1 onion, finely chopped

2 carrots, cut into dice

2 sticks of celery, cut into dice

300ml tomato passata

Grated zest of 1 lemon

1 tablespoon chopped parsley

2 cloves of garlic, finely grated

Serves 4

1 In a casserole that will hold the pieces of meat in a single layer, heat the oil and butter, season the veal with salt and pepper and dip lightly into flour.

2 Shake off the excess flour and put the pieces into the pan. Fry on both sides until each piece is mildly crusted and golden brown.

3 Remove from the pan and add the vegetables and cook until soft. Put the veal back into the pan and pour in the wine, allow to bubble up, then turn down the heat. Add the passata and chicken stock, cover and leave to braise slowly for about 1½ hours, by which time the meat will be melting tenderly.

4 All this can be done in advance and the veal reheated when needed, otherwise remove the veal and reduce the juices until slightly thick, pop the veal back in and add the parsley, garlic and lemon zest (which when all three are mixed together is called Gremolata). Serve with mashed potato, risotto or creamed polenta.

Risotto saffron

Ingredients

1 litre chicken stock

Sea salt and freshly ground black pepper

150g butter

2 tablespoons olive oil

1 red onion, finely chopped

300g risotto rice

1 tablespoon saffron threads

75ml vermouth

200g freshly grated Parmesan

1 Heat the chicken stock and add the saffron.

2 Melt 75g of the butter with the oil, add the onion and cook until very soft but not browned.

3 Add the rice and stir until all the grains become completely coated and season. Add the vermouth and two ladles of stock enough to cover. Stir and once the stock has been absorbed add more stock. Continue until all the stock has been used. At this point each grain should have a creamy coating but will remain *al dente*. Add the butter and the Parmesan, serve immediately.

Steak and chips

Steak and chips is still the nation's favourite meal. It's a special treat for most; it's certainly my first choice to cook for my wife and I on a rare night off at home and it's the original fast food, as it should not take more than 10 minutes to put together.

The most important thing about steak, and beef in general, is that it has to come from good cattle, and in Wales we are lucky to have our very own Welsh Black beef. Secondly, it has to be hung for at least three weeks, preferably more in the case of a good roast rib or sirloin.

When it comes to choosing the right steak for the right dish, it is to a certain extent a matter of individual choice. But there are a few things to remember: fillet steak is tops for tenderness but forgoes flavour. Sirloin (so called because the King knighted the loin) is the most common steak that you will come across and falls between the good flavour of my two favourites, rib eye and rump steak, and the texture of a buttery fillet.

Grilling – if you have gas barbeque make use of it in all weathers, grill outside and let the meat rest in a warm oven – produces a terrific crust on beef that contrasts well with a rosy red and juicy inside. For this reason, I have never understood the wish for a well done steak. I understand that the sight of underdone and bloody meat can be off-putting, but I would rather have a stew if I wanted well cooked meat. The most important thing about grilling steak is that the grill must be very hot and, when frying, the oil should be almost smoking before you put the steak in. And remember that resting meat after cooking, even a steak, is very important.

steak 'au poivre'

I have served steak au poivre since I took over Hilaire's kitchen from Simon Hopkinson whose recipe this basically is. When I took over Tyddyn Llan it went straight on the menu. One hotel inspector who ordered it asked where the garnish was, but to me it needs no garnish, just homemade chips and a crisp green salad.

Ingredients

2 tablespoons of black peppercorns

2 tablespoons of white peppercorns

4 175g fillet steaks or whatever your choice or budget

Salt

3 tablespoons of sunflower oil

75g unsalted butter

2 good slugs of brandy

6 tablespoons of meat glacé or ready made beef stock from a supermarket

Serves 4

1 Crush the peppercorns in a pestle or a coffee grinder. Tip the pepper into a sieve over a bowl and shake well to remove all the powdered pepper, use this for other seasoning. You can buy crushed peppercorns in the supermarket.

2 Press the peppercorns onto both sides of the steaks and place on a tray. Season with salt.

3 Heat the oil in a thick bottom frying pan, which is big enough to hold all the steaks without crowding, until hot. Place the steaks in the pan and fry for 2 minutes until a crust is formed. Turn the steaks and cook for a further 2 minutes. Do not have the heat so hot as to burn the pepper. If you require your meat more cooked turn the steaks again but resist turning too often.

4 Remove the steaks to a warm tray or plate and keep warm in a very low oven. Add 50g of the butter to the frying pan and allow to colour to a nut brown then add the brandy. Be careful if you are near curtains or your valuable vent above the cooker in case it ignites. Boil, scraping any bits from the bottom of the pan, add the cream, meat glacé or stock and bring to the boil.

5 Place the steaks on warm plates and add the remaining butter to the sauce and whisk, strain if you wish and pour over the steaks and serve with whatever you fancy. Steak au poivre also goes extremely well with shallot purée (page 197).

Game

From September until the end of January the local estates around Tyddyn Llan are busy with people tramping over their moorlands, gun in hand, and paying handsomely for the privilege of shooting partridges and pheasants – but probably without the faintest interest in what happens to their quarry after they have shot it. I am not a bloodsports man, I have to say. I like my birds dead, plucked and gutted on my chopping board. Flying birds actually scare me and to me Alfred Hitchcock's film *The Birds* is the most frightening film ever made. However I do love these shooting parties as they keep the restaurant busy during the winter. With the amount of wine consumed the night before the shooting I am not too sure how good anyone's aim is the next morning, so the pheasants and partridges do have a fair chance.

Game is the word to describe a bird or mammal that is hunted normally using a gun, for sport and for the table. Red leg partridges, pheasant, and the rare appearance of a woodcock, is just about all the game that that can be sourced locally, but the local shoots do very well out of these 'quality sport days' with syndicates, individuals and corporate clients. They also help the local hotels, although they shoot far more birds that we can use locally, which is why pheasants reach the shops at a reasonable price.

Grouse kicks off the game season on what has become known as the Glorious Twelfth (of August), followed at the beginning of September by partridge and wild duck becoming available. Pheasants start in October, as do woodcock, but it's rare to be offered any until December. They are never in abundance and, as chefs are always after them, they are always expensive.

There are two species of partridge: the red leg (French), which are plentiful at the local shoots, and the grey leg, known as the English, which to me are the better of the two. They're more expensive but they have a much finer taste.

While I like the taste of a wild rabbit in a fine casserole, it's not the type of dish to sit comfortably on the menu unless it's at lunchtime. But, taken off the bone, it is great mixed with some pasta or potato gnocchi.

The same goes for pigeon, apart from the French Bresse type (as mentioned in the chapter Signature Dishes). Wild pigeon, which do have an open season as they are considered to be a pest to the agricultural business, are very tasty, lean and cheap. A good way to use them is in salads as a starter.

I also like using venison, and hare, when it's available. As the venison season only closes for a few weeks you can get it during most of the year, but I would try and stay away from the farmed variety. While it does have the advantage of being consistently tender and young, to my mind it does not have the same flavour as the wild.

Braised venison with oranges

Ingredients

1 kg of boned and cubed venison

1 onion, chopped

2 carrots, diced

2 sticks of celery, diced

1 small bouquet garni containing thyme
   bay leaves and parsley stalks

150ml red wine

150ml white wine

150ml orange juice

50ml lemon juice

1 litre of chicken stock and ½ litre of beef
   stock if available

3 large oranges, blood if available, segmented

75g blackcurrants, frozen will do

Cooked wild mushrooms to garnish

Sunflower oil

Salt and pepper

Serves 6

1 In a large casserole pan heat the oil. When hot add the venison in small batches and fry until coloured, season with salt and pepper. Remove from the pan onto a tray.

2 Add more oil if necessary and sweat the onions, carrots and celery for 5 minutes without colouring.

3 Return the venison to the pan and add the wines, bring to the boil and reduce by half. Add the orange and lemon juices with the bouquet garni, cover with the stocks or water and simmer for about 1 hour and 10 minutes or until tender.

4 When the meat is cooked remove the pieces of venison with a slotted spoon onto a tray and cover with cling film.

5 Reduce the juices until they thicken slightly into a sauce, return the meat to the sauce. Check seasoning.

6 Add the orange segments and the blackcurrants along with the wild mushrooms if using. Serve with mashed potatoes or creamed polenta.

Game terrine

Ingredients

500g of mixed game meats
250g sausage meat
350g foie gras
5 chopped shallots
3 chopped cloves of garlic
½ teaspoon of green peppercorns
½ chopped truffle [optional]
Madeira and Calvados
250g breast of pheasant, pigeon or grouse
Italian back fat or streaky bacon
Fresh thyme
Salt and pepper

Serves 10-12

1 Cook the shallots and garlic in butter until soft.

2 Wrap the breasts in thinly sliced fat.

3 Mince the game meats, sausage and foie gras with the shallots, garlic and thyme. Season with salt and pepper.

4 Add the peppercorns and chopped truffles.

5 Line two terrines with thinly sliced fat or bacon overlapping the sides.

6 Fill the terrines with the mixture placing the breasts in the centre.

7 Cover with foil and bake in a deep tray with water at 180°C for 1 hour and 20 minutes or until firm to the touch.

8 Leave to cool for at least a day.

Pot roast pheasant with port and juniper

Ingredients

2 large hen pheasants, plucked and hung
   for 5-7 days
Vegetable oil
1 medium onion, finely chopped
1 carrot, finely chopped
2 sticks celery, finely chopped
3 large leeks, diced
500ml red wine
50ml port
500ml chicken or veal stock
bouquet garni – fresh parsley, thyme and bay
10 juniper berries
Salt and pepper to taste

Serves 4

1 Trim pheasants of excess fat in body cavity. Heat a little oil in a cast-iron casserole and seal pheasants thoroughly, turning carefully until the entire outside is light golden brown. Remove from pan and keep warm.

2 Add onion, carrot and celery to the same pan and cook for 2 minutes.

3 Add leeks and cook for further 2 minutes over brisk heat. Season with salt and pepper.

4 Add red wine and port and reduce to half, then add stock, bouquet garni and berries.

5 Return pheasants to cooking pan, check seasoning, cover and cook in a slow oven, 170°C for 35 mins until tender. Strain and reduce to a sauce. Pour off all fat from the pan.

6 Remove bouquet garni and press through a sieve to make a smooth sauce. Carve the pheasant and serve with seasonal vegetables.

Pappardelle with hare sauce

Ingredients

The legs and shoulders from a hare plus all
the bones.

300g fresh or good quality dried Pappardelle

½ bottle of red wine

A bouquet garni

1 onion

2 large carrots

3 celery sticks

4 cloves

1 orange

500ml chicken stock

10g dark chocolate

Salt and pepper

Freshly grated Parmesan

1 Heat some sunflower oil in a saucepan
and seal and colour the pieces of hare, season
with salt and pepper, remove to a tray and
continue until all the hare is coloured.

2 Chop all the vegetables and add to the pan,
cook until they begin to soften, add the red wine
and put the pieces of hare back in. Bring to
the boil for a few minutes, then add the stock
and water to cover. Add the bouquet garni, the
orange cut in half and squeezed, the cloves and
simmer for at least an hour. Some pieces might
take longer, but you want all the flesh to be soft.

3 Leave to cool and remove all the meat
from the bones, strain the sauce into a clean
saucepan and reduce so that it thickens slightly.
Add the meat broken up into small pieces. This
can be done a day or so in advance.

4 Cook the pasta in plenty of boiling salted
water, drain, reheat the hare sauce while the
pasta is cooking at the last moment before
mixing with the pasta. Add the chocolate and
shake the pan to mix the sauce, add to the pasta
and serve with the Parmesan on the side.

Roast woodcock

Woodcock is a very special bird, to me only
second to a grouse, but so much harder to get.
The only time I can remember using it on a
regular menu was when I was working at the
Drangway. Colin Pressdee knew someone who
must have been a great shot because he kept
us regularly supplied. Colin devised a recipe,
and I think original for the time which was the
novelle cuisine era, of half a bird served pink
with strips of root vegetables in a pastry case
and a raspberry vinegar, based stock reduction
sauce. For its time it was an inventive dish.

At Tyddyn Llan we are sometimes given
woodcock from shooters who stay and my
favourite way of cooking them is to simply
roast them – not even gutted – topped with
some butter, salt and pepper. When just pink,
scrape out the livers and heart and spread
these onto some crisp croutons. Pour a touch
of brandy into the roasting pan, then add a
dash of stock. Carve the birds and eat; either
eat a whole one as a main course or share it
as a starter. Simple, but so good when you
can get hold of them.

Grouse

During the first weeks after the Glorious Twelfth, grouse can be extremely expensive. It is never cheap but by September it has at least become an affordable luxury. The price of two grouse and a good bottle of Burgundy is less than you would pay for an inexpensive and mediocre meal in a restaurant and grouse is not difficult to cook. As long as it is turned and basted a few times so that it cooks evenly, and left pink but not rare, it is a tolerant bird whose flavour cannot be spoiled even by the clumsiest cook.

If there is any skill in preparing grouse it is in choosing the right bird. I must admit that sometimes a few have come to me that were a little on the tough side and were turned into a terrine. Hold the bird by its beak, and if it does not break it will be tough, but, really, faith should be invested in the butcher or game dealer.

I was taught how to cook grouse by Colin Pressdee, who knew better than to muck around with grouse. He kept it simple, just serving it with some bread sauce, breadcrumbs fried in butter or some fried bread topped with the bird's cooked liver, game chips and gravy. This is not just my favourite way of cooking and eating this magnificent bird, it is my desert island dinner, preferably preceded by half a native lobster and followed by a perfect crème brulée.

Roast grouse

Ingredients

2 young grouse
50g unsalted butter
Salt and pepper
2 slices of streaky bacon
2 sprigs of thyme
2 bay leaves
1 small chopped shallot

Bread sauce

400ml milk
1 tablespoon chopped onion
2 cloves
A few parsley stalks
2 sprigs of thyme
4 slices of white bread, crusts removed and
    made into breadcrumbs
30g butter

Game chips

2 Maris Piper potatoes
Vegetable oil for deep frying

Gravy

Half a glass of red wine (about 50ml)
A slug of brandy
200ml strong chicken stock

Braised Savoy cabbage

1 small Savoy cabbage
3 shallots, cut in half and slice thinly
4 slices of streaky bacon, cut into thin strips
50g butter

Serves 2

1 Remove the wing bone and the wishbone making sure that the skin covers all the flesh. Make a small cut into the bottom of the legs and holding the feet twist and pull and all the sinew will come out.

2 Season the birds inside with salt and pepper and place a sprig of thyme and a bay leaf inside the cavity, smear the breasts with butter and lay a slice of streaky bacon cut in half on top.

3 Preheat the oven to 220°C.

4 Roast the grouse for about 15 minutes turning and basting three times, remove from the oven and leave to rest for 10 minutes on a warm plate. Put the wine and brandy into the roast tray and scrape up all the juices, pour in the stock and boil to a thin gravy, strain and keep warm.

5 Serve with game chips, bread sauce, a sprig of watercress and some redcurrant jelly (I would recommend the Welsh Lady brand, it is excellent).

Bread sauce

1 Put all the ingredients except the breadcrumbs and butter into a saucepan and bring to a simmer, take off the heat and leave to infuse for a while.

2 Strain the milk into a clean pan, add the breadcrumbs and stir with a whisk over a low heat until it starts to thicken. Add the butter and season with salt and pepper. If it's too thick add a little more milk.

Game Chips

1 Slice the potatoes as thinly as possible on a mandoline as for crisps, and place in a container under running water for half an hour to remove the starch.

2 Drain and dry well and deep fry in hot oil until golden brown, drain on kitchen paper and season with salt. (Do what I have done many times at home – reheat Kettle crisps on a tray in a warm oven) no one will know the difference!

Braised Cabbage

1 Quarter the cabbage and remove the core, slice thinly, melt the butter, sweat the shallots until soft, add the bacon and cook for a few minutes.

2 Add the cabbage and stir well, barely cover with water and simmer until the cabbage has a slight bite left to it. Season with salt and pepper.

Food heroes

Over the past 30 years lots of people and restaurants have made a lasting impression on me. I can still recall the first time I was taken to the Waterside Inn in the late 70s; the time I nervously took my girlfriend to Sharrow Bay at the age of 18; my first meal cooked by Alastair Little, the master of modern British cooking; my first cookbook *Cuisine Gourmande* by Michel Guérard, that blew me away and possibly the book that has influenced me more in my life in cookery than any other. All the happy family times at the Walnut Tree, the time when travelling around France and dining at Paul Bocuse where my only credit card would not work and the many times I drag my wife around the markets of the world.

My food heroes have all been a great influence on me in one way or another, and at this point I must say a huge thank you to Danny and Bettie Murphy who at the age of 24 gave me the chance to move to London and run their restaurant kitchen and for those two years gave me their full support.

You may not recognise all my heroes but they are amazing people in the restaurant world. It's not saying that the current tops chefs such as Gordon Ramsay, Marco Pierre White and Richard Corrigan are not heroes but I feel they are friends and colleagues as well as being great chefs.

Sonia Blech

When I was 15 and still in school, and all my mates were going for job interviews to be electricians, plumbers, car mechanics or builders, I knew those types of job were not for me. The threat from my Dad – 'It's okay if you fail your exams, there's always a job down the pit' – made me study and pass my exams, and when two jobs for a trainee chef appeared on the school notice board I applied to both of them. The careers office came back saying that both positions were taken, but there was another one at the Crown at Whitebrook. Mum and Dad took me for the interview and all seemed well. The job was offered. I could not start for another three months, until I finished school, but they were prepared to wait and I was so pleased. And what a lucky boy I was, as it turned out this restaurant was the only restaurant in Wales to be the proud holder of a Michelin star. What a great start.

My first day was an eye opener and I loved it. There was lots of washing up but there was lots to learn. I remember the first time Sonia showed me how to chop an onion, fillet a fish or prepare a rack of lamb. During the two years I worked with Mr and Mrs Blech I learnt so much. Sonia had lots of patience and I can never thank her enough for all she taught me. She inspired me and gave me the great passion for being a chef.

Sonia's food moved on after the Crown days, and for 15 years she ran a successful restaurant in London called Mijanou, where her food style was very definitive and inventive. But I still look back with fondness at the simple, classic food served at the Crown in the 70s. I have known Sonia and Neville for 30 years now and have been honoured to have cooked for them on many of their special occasions. Over the years they have both helped my career so much, and when I needed money to buy my first restaurant they were there to help. They were shareholders in Hilaire all the way though, and when I could not afford to buy wines for Tyddyn Llan, Neville installed an awesome wine list and has constantly helped with its development.

I remember the first time Sonia showed me how to chop an onion

Venison with elderberry and juniper sauce

Of all the dishes that Sonia cooked while I worked alongside her at the Crown, this is the one that always reappears on my menus when a good saddle of venison arrives. Sometimes I pair the pink slices of the saddle with a chunk of the shin of venison cut into an osso bucco. This way you also let more flavour into the sauce.

Ingredients

1 saddle of venison, completly trimmed like a fillet

As many venison bones and trimmings as possible

½ bottle of red wine

100ml port

A mirepoix of 2 chopped onions, 4 carrots and 2 celery sticks

1 bouquet garni

2 tablespoons of elderberry jelly

2 tablespoons of Forum red wine vinegar

10 crushed juniper berries

500ml chicken stock

500ml veal stock

Serves 4

1 Roast the bones and trimmings until a golden brown.

2 Into a clean saucepan pour any fat that is in the roasting tray and add the mirepoix, cook until soft and lightly coloured. Add the bones and trimmings, pour half the wine into the pan and the rest into the roasting tray. Scrape all that is stuck to the tray and transfer to the saucepan, reduce the wine by half.

3 Add the two stocks, bouquet garni, juniper berries and cover with water. Bring to the boil and remove any scum that comes to the top. Lower the heat to a simmer and cook for 1 hour.

4 In a separate pan boil the vinegar and jelly together, ready to pour into the sauce at the end.

5 Strain the sauce into a clean pan and reduce removing any scum as it rises to the surface until the sauce is slightly thick. You can cool the sauce down and it will keep in the fridge for up to a week.

6 To cook and serve; preheat the oven to 220°C and into a hot frying pan add a small amount of oil and seal the fillet of venison an all sides until golden. Place into the oven for about 8 minutes for medium rare, reheat the sauce and the garnish that you are serving. Cabbage parcel, polenta, wild mushrooms or braised butter beans are good to go with the venison.

7 Remove the venison from the oven, place onto a warm plate or tray and keep warm while pouring away any fat from the pan. Pour in the port and boil to a syrup, than add the sauce and reduce to a coating thickness but not sticky. All this is happening while the meat is resting.

8 Arrange the garnish on four heated plates, slice the venison into three or four slices per person and pour the sauce over.

Franco Taruschio

For over 39 years The Walnut Tree Inn, a few miles outside Abergavenny, was an institution and a foodies' paradise, Ann and Franco Taruschio ran the place with passion and tremendous energy it was such a special place and every time I was visiting my mum at home, lunch or dinner was a priority. The place had such a special atmosphere and you always left feeling that a good time was had by all although the some 40-minute drive back home to Mum's was sometime a little edgy for the driver with three merry passengers to contend with.

It was at the Walnut Tree I first ever saw a fresh truffle but not just one, boxes of aromatic white truffles which Franco served to me with beautiful light Tagliatelle and lashings of the fine truffle on top. The lasagne was legendary and in later years the Vincisgrassi became Susan's and my favourite pasta dish of all time. Franco's play with Nouvelle Cuisine gave us dishes of smoked salmon Bavarois and strawberry soup. When they adopted their Thai daughter, Franco was the first ever to put far eastern influences onto his menu with goujonettes of Sole and Thai dip or the wonderful spicy Thai pork appetizer. It was the classic Italian dishes where Franco's cooking inspired many chefs; such as huge bowls of steaming brodetto (a fish stew), the thick slice of freshly roasted porchetta, Piedmontese peppers and no visit would be complete without a plate of home cured Bresoala and crescente. All of these have appeared on my menus somewhere in the past years. Franco's approach to running a restaurant and style of cooking has been a great influence to me over 30 years, I even celebrated my 21st and 40th birthday there but after 39 years they sold and sort of retired, but there are still the books, memories and Franco on the other end of a telephone line if you ever need advice.

Vincisgrassi

Vincisgrassi has been described by our customers as the best pasta dish they have ever eaten, which is a great compliment to me as I am not Italian but Welsh. All I do is follow the recipe from Franco and Ann Taruschio's first cookbook, *Leaves from the Walnut Tree*. Franco does, as well. I remember when he cooked for a special dinner at Tyddyn Llan he asked for his book and followed the recipe.

Vincisgrassi is a speciality of the Marche region of Italy, in particular of Macerata where Franco comes from. It was named after an Austrian general, Windisch Graets, who was with his troops in Ancona in 1799 during the Napoleonic war. Actually Antonio Nebbia, who wrote a gastronomic manual in 1784, mentioned in his book a similar dish called Princisgras.

Vincisgrassi was on the famous Walnut Tree menu for 20 years. It is a classic, and is not that difficult to make. You could always cheat by buying readymade sheets of pasta, but you do need cèpes. Frozen ones will work well as long as your frying pan is very hot when you cook them. I have even made it successfully using chestnut or flat mushrooms with a few dried cèpes added to them. If it was a very grand occasion the finished dish would have shavings of fresh white truffles over the top, but at the moment they are priced at £2,500 a kilo so make do with a few splashes of truffle oil.

Vincisgrassi

Ingredients

Pasta

500g strong plain flour
2 whole eggs plus 4 egg yolks
1 teaspoon salt

Sauce

400g sliced cèpes
200g Parma ham or Carmarthen ham, cut into julienne (thin strips)
1 litre milk
60g flour
150g butter
200g single cream
60ml extra virgin olive oil
3 tablespoons finely chopped parsley
salt and freshly ground black pepper
150g grated Parmesan cheese

Serves 6 as a main, 10 as a starter

1 Make a dough from the pasta ingredients, knead well and roll through a pasta machine as you would for lasagne. Cut the pasta lengths into squares approx. 12.5cm square. Cook the squares in plenty of boiling salted water, a few at a time. Place on linen cloths to drain.

2 For the sauce. Melt 50g of the butter, add the flour and blend in well. Add the milk, which has been previously heated, a little at a time beating well with a balloon whisk. Cook the cèpes in the olive oil and add to the sauce. Stir in the ham. Add the cream and parsley, season and bring to the boil. Turn off the heat.

3 To assemble the vincisgrassi butter a gratin dish and cover the bottom with a layer of pasta, then spread over a layer of sauce, dot with butter and sprinkle with some Parmesan cheese. Continue the process making layer after layer, finishing with a sauce layer and a sprinkling of Parmesan cheese. Cook in an oven preheated to 200°C for 20 minutes.

Colin Pressdee

I first met Colin at The Crown at Whitebrook during one of Sonia Blech's gastronomic evenings way back in 1976, then two very good customers suggested visiting Colin's restaurant in Swansea. I remember it well, I loved the place and the different approach to cooking. The night went on and on and I remember leaving at around 3am. This was in June, so after the 90-minute drive home it was daylight and I was on breakfast duty.

I applied for a job and started in the October. The first Saturday was a very special dinner with Michel Roux as the guest of honour, and Colin served straightforward, excellent food: a platter of seafood weighed down with oysters, clams, crabs and langoustine, followed by poached turbot on the bone with a classic beurre blanc, roast pheasant for mains, followed by cheese and a kiwi fruit salad for dessert. Colin was no chef patisserie and this fruit was new to this country but it was still a special way to round off the meal.

For the next four years I loved working at the Drangway. Colin was a great boss and all though my own career as a boss I have always tried to be as good as he was back in the old days of the Drangway. During those four years I learnt everything I know about seafood. Turbot and bass would be delivered by the stone, crab and lobster straight from the Gower coast, and oysters kept in special tanks at the back of the kitchen. And, of course there was the laverbread freshly picked by Colin himself. He was very much into Nouvelle Cuisine at the time, but rather than pretty pictures on a plate it was light, super fresh food on a plate. No fuss, great taste; that's Colin.

Oysters

This is a dish that's been on my menus in London and in Wales for the past 20 years. Oysters are not to everyone's taste, but once hooked this dish keeps regulars coming back for more.

If oysters are not for you, try a variation on this dish by adding to a buttered gratin dish a layer of laverbread, then a layer of cockles, mussels and prawns, all topped with the creamy Stilton mix, and baked in the oven until golden. It would make an excellent starter at the next dinner party or a light lunch with a crisp green salad. If shellfish is totally out, replace with good quality canned tuna. Even the children will love laverbread this way and it's full of vitamins!

Oysters 'au gratin'

with laverbread and stilton

Ingredients

5 or 6 freshly opened oysters on half a shell
    per person
1 tin of laverbread or fresh
100g Stilton grated
300g full fat cream cheese
Lemon in wedges

Serves 6

1 Cream the Stilton and cream cheese in a food processor.

2 Put a teaspoon of laverbread in each shell and place an oyster on top.

3 Carefully cover each oyster with the cheese mix and tightly place onto a tray so that they do not slide over, at this stage you can refrigerate until needed.

4 Pre heat oven to 200°C.

5 Place in the oven for 8 minutes when the cheese should be golden brown and bubbling.

6 Place the oysters onto plates but be careful as they will be hot, (maybe use a pair of kitchen gloves until you develop chef's asbestos hands) serve with a wedge of lemon.

Simon Hopkinson

For 12 years between 1983 and 1995 Simon Hopkinson was one of the finest chefs cooking in London, and together with Rowley Leigh and Alastair Little, epitomised the style of cooking that had the greatest influence on me when I, after many years following the latest trends, was searching for my own style and direction.

Simon was the chef who opened Hilaire back in 1983 with the backing of a small company called Kennedy Brooks. Almost straight away, with Simon's straight to the point, bold flavours and precise cooking, Hilaire was London's hottest restaurant and so it continued until he left in June 1987, when yours truly took over. Being asked if I was interested in taking the job was an honour. The first interview was with Simon and straight away it felt that I was on the same wavelength as him. My one regret was that I was not able to work alongside him before taking over, due to my commitments at Café Rouge.

Simon moved to Bibendum, 10 minutes walk away. The dining room at Bibendum is in my view still the most beautiful restaurant setting in London, and it was where for the next seven years he produced some amazing food. Still today I look back on this time for ideas that can be used on my menus.

Simon's classic steak au poivre is now my classic; his rabbit leg is the same but mine is stuffed with black pudding; his method of confit I still follow today and his taste in desserts are a heavy influence on my menu. Bibendum is also special as it was the location of Susan's and my first date, the place we had lunch before getting married and where we celebrated the eve of the next century.

Simon has gone on to write some brilliant books. I have been through three copies of the first one because it has been used so much and fallen apart. It was voted the most useful cookbook ever which I agree with. It's a shame we cannot taste his cooking anymore but at least we can read and observe his ideas and passion.

Almonds

Almond tart is one of the easiest tarts to make. It has a similarity in ingredients with a traditional Bakewell tart, but is not as rich. You can use any flavour of jam on the bottom, or fresh cherries, dried apricots or one of my favourites, prunes. Try and find good quality nuts. We buy Spanish blanched Marcona almonds and grind them ourselves for the tart.

Almond tart

Ingredients

1 batch of shortcrust pastry (see page 128)

100g softened butter

100g caster sugar

2 large free range eggs

50g ground almonds

50g whole blanched almonds, ground in a
food processor

20g flaked almonds

2 tablespoons of jam of your choice or 150g
of semi dried prunes or apricots

1 egg, lightly beaten

Serves 10-12

1 Pre heat the oven to 180°C.

2 Roll out the pastry as thinly as possible and line a loose bottomed 20cm x 4cm tart tin. Line the pastry with a large sheet of greaseproof paper or tin foil and fill with baking beans or any dried pulses such as haricot beans. Leave to rest for 20 minutes and then bake for 20 minutes. Remove from the oven and take out the foil or paper with the beans and keep for future use. Brush the base with beaten egg to form a seal and bake for a further 5 minutes.

3 Turn the oven temperature down to 150°C.

4 For the filling beat together the butter and sugar in an electric mixer until light and fluffy. Add one egg and continue beating then add the other egg and beat again until entirely incorporated. Add the two types of ground almonds and carefully fold them in.

5 Spoon the jam or place the fruits onto the base of the pastry case and fill with the almond mix, sprinkle with the flaked almonds and bake for 1 hour and 10 minutes. Switch off the oven and leave to cool with the door ajar for 15 minutes; it is best served warm with some thick cream.

Rowley Leigh

Rowley Leigh was the chef who opened the big, brash and busy Kensington Place, the first mega big restaurant. One hundred covers was considered to be big back in 1987. The place was highly unpretentious and bustling, serving what was labelled modern British cooking. I ate at K.P. more times than any other London restaurant – probably weekly at times – and it always amazed me how they managed to serve so many punters excellent inventive food.

Over the years some great classic dishes came out of the kitchen: the chicken and goats' cheese mousse, vinaigrette of red peppers, scallops with pea purée and griddled foie gras on sweet corn pancake, and of course the famous grand assiette of desserts. I have amassed a huge collection of menus over the years which are a great reference when looking for ideas, especially as they are all dated and they closely follow the seasons. The food at K.P. was always good and every year I would look forward to having roast grouse cooked by someone else. Somehow it always tastes better.

I do not know Rowley on a personal level but through the entertaining columns he wrote during the late 90s for *The Guardian* and through the many meals he cooked or supervised he has made a big impression on my outlook on food.

Rowley has now moved on and opened an even bigger French style brasserie/rotisserie with classic food; everyone wants to eat at the Café Anglais in Bayswater.

Pineapple

Marco Pierre White, the first British chef to ever be awarded three Michelin stars, created a sumptuous pineapple recipe which brought a heroic conclusion to a meal at his restaurant. The roast fruit was immaculately peeled with each eye removed and replaced with shards of vanilla, and stood on a silver salver with its crown of leaves in place, surrounded by aromatic roasting juices, spiked with chilli and served with a mascarpone ice cream. It was a great dish.

From Marco's idea, Rowley Leigh came up with grilled pineapple with chilli syrup and coconut sorbet, which has also found its way on to the menu at Tyddyn Llan. The idea may sound crazy but it's not if you can remember back to the 70s when the waiter would fry slices of pineapple with pepper and flambé it in front of you. Talking of the 70s, do you remember the curling gammon steak with tinned pineapple ring that used to be a staple of British catering?

When you peel a pineapple use a long serrated knife and make a clean slice across the base and the top of the pineapple, so that the stalk is removed and the fruit sits firmly on the board. Following the contours, trim away the skin from the top to bottom but do not try to remove the eyes. Cut grooves either side of the eyes diagonally from top to bottom, so that two double tracks crisscross around each eye, then lift out each eye with the point of a potato peeler or with the twist of a small sharp knife.

Grilled pineapple with chilli and coconut sorbet

Ingredients

1 ripe pineapple

For the Chilli syrup

2 red chillies, medium strength
1 vanilla pod
3 star anise
100g caster sugar
1 bay leaf
150ml water
25ml dark rum

For the Sorbet

250ml water
500g coconut purée
Juice of ½ lemon

Serves 4

1 Split the chillies – wearing rubber gloves unless intrepid – and remove the seeds under the cold tap. Cut the chillies into very fine, short strips. Split the vanilla pod in half and place in a saucepan with the sugar, chillies, star anise, bay leaf and water. Simmer very gently for 30 minutes, diluting with a little cold water if the mixture gets too thick and sticky.

2 Peel the pineapple and slice lengthways into four. Cut away the stalky centre and cut each segment into three or four long, thin rectangular slices, then lift them out and place on a sheet of foil on a grill tray. Place under a very hot grill for 3 or 4 minutes until golden brown. Serve the pineapple piping hot with some of the chilli syrup with a portion of the sorbet in a little dish besides it.

3 For the sorbet: I am sorry but there is no substitute for using an ice cream machine with this recipe, and you'll have to visit a high class deli to find coconut purée, otherwise do some judicious shopping in the frozen food aisle. Simple – dissolve the sugar in the water, add the coconut purée and lemon juice, freeze in an ice cream machine.

shaun Hill

Shaun Hill is the gentlemen of chefs. He always seems cool and calm and has served me with many wonderful meals at both Gidleigh Park a country house hotel on Dartmoor in Devon and the Merchant House in Ludlow and I cannot think of a time when I have not left his restaurant without lots of inspiration and ideas. Oh, and having drunk too much wine.

Shaun's cooking is classic French cuisine but he applies the flavours of the Orient, Middle East and the Mediterranean. His style is simple as he cooks alone and not with the help of a big brigade, so what you get is Shaun personally cooking for you. I think I have modelled myself on Shaun in a lot of ways as I also cook every dish myself, with the help of two young local boys. I am not one for television appearances and the big publicity machine. I would like to think that we have both earned our respect from the food that we have put onto our plates.

During our first year at Tyddyn Llan I worked completely alone in the kitchen for many days with Susan serving the guests. Together we would share the washing up, and on many occasions at the end of service I thought to myself how does Shaun do it? Believe me, it was not easy and my respect for Shaun became even greater.

Many of Shaun's dishes have been noted on my menus such as his scallops with lentils and coriander, and his potato and olive cake. When he moved to Ludlow from the grand surroundings of Gidleigh I for one could not understand it, but within a few years there were three top restaurants in the small market town and a daily market of the finest local produce. The town became a foodie paradise and I feel a lot of it was down to Shaun. I hope that I can continue to cook and develop in the same way as Shaun did until he sold up and moved on. These days Shaun has consultancy work in London and Worcester, and has taken over the famous Walnut Tree.

classic French cuisine with flavours of the Orient, Middle East and the Mediterranean

sautéed langoustine
with chick pea, coriander and olive oil

Ingredients

24 langoustine or king prawns
100g chick peas, soaked over night
4 shallots
2 cloves
1 teaspoon ground cinnamon
1 teaspoon ground coriander
1 teaspoon ground cumin
1 lemon
200ml fish stock
100ml olive oil
Pinch of saffron
3 tablespoons of passata
1 tablespoon chopped coriander
50g butter
Salt and pepper

Serves 4

1 Fry the shallots in a little olive oil for a few minutes but do not colour. Add the garlic and spices and cook for another minute. Add the chick peas and two slices of lemon.

2 Pour the fish stock over, add the passata and bring to a simmer for 30 minutes.

3 Remove the slices of lemon and throw away. Take out about four tablespoons of the chick peas and set aside, purée the sauce in a blender, and add some lemon juice and season with salt and pepper. Keep until required.

4 Very gently heat the prawns in the butter, reheat the sauce and whisk in the olive oil, add the reserved chick peas and chopped coriander.

5 Spoon the sauce onto four warm plates and top with six langoustine each.

Sally Clarke

I have always been in awe of Sally Clarke. I am not sure if it's the lady in authority thing or the respect I have for her as a brilliant restaurateur and businesswoman. As a chef for the past 22 years she has produced the finest and most seasonal menus you will come across. Her shop next to the restaurant is a dream and the bread from her bakery supplies the finest restaurants and shops in London, but a table for lunch is always a delight.

Sally's style is unpretentious and stylish, freshness on a plate. The flavours just stand out. I always remember one particular lunch dish of roasted cherry tomatoes on the vine with a Tapenade Crostini and the most amazing buffalo mozzarella I had ever tasted. Sally later told me it was flown directly from Naples once a week and it has been on my menu ever since.

Clarke's bakery supplied Hilaire daily with their wonderful bread. They produce 25 different types of bread, rolls, croissants and brioche seven days a week. The shop next door sells cheese from Neal's Yard Dairy, Californian wines, chocolate truffles that are to die for and a huge range of savoury and sweet tarts that would grace any home buffet with elegant style. It's a route I have taken many times for a party at home.

Bread

Bread is one of everyone's staple foods, one item that we will eat for breakfast, lunch and dinner and of course as the great snack, a sandwich. My wife unfortunately cannot eat wheat so this great pleasure is no longer for her and she really moans when I make some toast at home, the smell really gets to her. I have tried making bread with gluten free flour but it would have been better to use the loaves for an extension to the hotel.

Bread making is easy, you just need time and a reliable oven. Homemade bread is just flour, yeast, salt and water where a typical shop bought loaf contains wheat flour, yeast, water, wheat protein, salt, vinegar, dextrose, soya flour, vegetable fat, emulsifier, E472, a flour treatment agent E300 and a preservative to inhibit mould growth, so it's easy to work out which is best for you.

Apart from my early days of cooking over 30 years ago my bread making skills laid dormant for many years until I came to Tyddyn Llan. The kitchen at Hilaire in London was very busy and unsuitable for making bread due to lack of space and unreliable ovens. But we did serve some of the best bread in London, I have always believed that if you can buy better than you can make it, do so; our bread came from Clarke's, a bakery and restaurant run by one of the best lady chefs in this country, Sally Clarke, so when I took over the restaurant in Wales who better to turn to for bread recipes than the great lady herself. Most of the recipes are now available in Sally's book which is available in hard and soft back.

Country style bread

Ingredients

500g strong white flour
15g of salt
15g of fresh yeast
300ml of warm water

1 Mix the water and yeast together, add the salt to the flour and on a slow speed with a dough hook attachment mix the water and yeast into the flour.

2 Continue to mix for 5 to 8 minutes until the dough is smooth. Cover with a damp cloth and leave in a warm place to prove, this may take up to an hour.

3 Place the dough on a clean table and knead again to expel any air. Shape into two round loaves or into four baguettes, place onto a baking tray and bake in a hot oven 200°C for 25 minutes for the loaves or 15 minutes for the baguettes until it is crisp and golden and sounds hollow when the base is knocked.

Hazelnut and raisin bread

Ingredients

400g strong white flour
100g rye flour
10g salt
15g yeast
300ml water
180g hazelnuts
100g raisins

1 Mix the water and yeast together and put all the dry ingredients in a mixing bowl.

2 Proceed as the first recipe but just rolling into two loaves. Some times they may need an extra 5 minutes cooking time.

Granary bread with four seeds

Ingredients

300g wholemeal flour
200g white flour
1 tablespoon of sunflower seeds
1 tablespoon of pumpkin seeds
10g salt
10g fresh yeast
1 teaspoon of honey
300ml warm water
1 teaspoon of sesame seeds
1 teaspoon of poppy seeds

1 Mix all the dry ingredients together except the sesame and poppy seeds.

2 Mix the honey, water and yeast together, mix with the dry ingredients and process as the first recipe. Before leaving the loaves to prove, sprinkle with the sesame and poppy seeds.

Focaccia

Ingredients

500g strong white flour
10g salt
20g yeast
250ml warm water
100ml olive oil
Chopped rosemary
Maldon sea salt for sprinkling

1 Mix the yeast and water together, add the olive oil and mix into the flour with the salt. Mix and prove, then roll out to about 2cm thickness. Push your fingers into the flat dough, sprinkle with a little sea salt and rosemary and drizzle a little olive oil over the top. Leave to prove and bake at 200°C until golden, which should take about 20 minutes.

Breadsticks

Ingredients

200g of focaccia dough (see previous page)
50g of finely grated Parmesan
Olive oil

1 Take 200g of the focaccia mix and add 50g of finely grated Parmesan and a dash of olive oil. Divide into four pieces.

2 Roll out on a floured table until thin enough to roll though a pasta machine, keep rolling though the machine until the fourth setting then roll though the tagliatelle cutter, carefully lay out on baking trays and leave to prove for 10 minutes. Bake at 180°C for around 8 minutes, check regularly as they can easily burn with amount of cheese in them.

Alice Walters

For over 20 years a lady I have never met has been a huge influence over the way I cook. It all started when Clarissa Dickson Wright, who was working at the Books for Cooks shop in Notting Hill Gate at the time, recommended a Chez Panisse cookbook when I asked her for inspiration. That copy is now battered and falling to pieces, but it stopped me from trying to emulate the great Michelin starred chefs of France and Great Britain – none of whom I had ever worked for – and encouraged me to think for myself and develop my own style which ever since the 80s has been led by produce and the seasons.

It took until my 40th birthday in the year 2000 for me to actually get to Chez Panisse. Sally Clarke booked me a table for dinner and also insisted that the following day I return for lunch in the café upstairs. Although I felt that Sally's time for dinner – at 5.30pm – was a little early she was completely right. After a flight from London I proudly walked though the door of Chez Panisse. The chef at the time was Christopher Lee, who gave us a fantastic tour of the whole place and explained how it all operated. The food was amazingly good and so simple. The following day in the café we had lunch of the most amazing tasting tomato salad ever using heirloom and cherry tomatoes, perfectly slow-cooked king salmon with summer beans and olive oil, a pizzetta of goats cheese and salad leaves and their famous Sauternes and olive oil cake with strawberries and cream.

The place was packed and buzzing, and since the first trip I have been lucky enough to have returned a dozen times and always found everything about the place living up to my expectation – with the exception of the fact that I never met the lady herself.

What is so amazing about Alice Walters is that, in general terms, she is no chef. Yes, when she cooks, she does so wonderfully, but with reluctance and has only occasionally run the kitchen at Chez Panisse. She's no business women either. It took nearly 30 years for the restaurant to make a profit. There are no Chez Panisse sites in Vegas, or London, or anywhere else and there are no frozen pizzas with the name Chez Panisse on them. But with eight books, hundreds of talks, dozens of honours and awards, and her own foundation she is my heroine, and America's heroine, for the way she has transformed the way many Americans eat and the way they think about food.

California

a huge
influence over
the way I cook

Running a hotel

Breakfast

For two years I worked in a wonderful part of Scotland, in the south west corner in a town called Newton Stewart, where I made some wonderful friends who I remain in touch with to this very day.

The Kirroughtree Hotel, on the outskirts of the town, was regarded as one of the finest in the area and it was where I worked for two very happy years. The only drawback was breakfast. Having cooked breakfast at the Crown Inn it was not one of my favourite jobs, but here I was back cooking the eggs and bacon in Scotland three to four days a week. When I left Scotland for London I thought 'No more breakfasts'. I did not ever want to work in a hotel again, until of course Susan and I happened to buy Tyddyn Llan. Since day one, with the very rare exception I have been at the stove every morning to cook breakfast for our guests before they depart.

As with everything we cook at Tyddyn Llan, all our breakfast products are made from the very best ingredients, from dry cured bacon, pork and leek sausages and black pudding from Edwards of Conwy, and eggs from local farms, though to natural smoked haddock and the finest smoked salmon. Laverbread is also always on offer to accompany the bacon, and so are cockles, which is a tradition from South Wales.

One popular dish is laverbread in an overcoat, either topped with crisp streaky bacon or smoked salmon. The only things I do not cook and do not appear on the breakfast menu are kippers. It's not that I have anything against them, it's just that with too much to choose from you never know when they are going to sell. Baked beans are another omission, for the obvious reasons, plus also Susan cannot stand the smell.

Susan and I feel that breakfast is just as important as lunch or dinner. It has to be right as it the last impression the guest has before leaving and parting with their hard earned cash.

People are surprised that it's me cooking their breakfast, but to be honest I love doing it. It also gets me out of bed in the morning. The thought of early guests from a shooting party waiting while my sausages are not ready is enough to get anyone out of bed. The art to serving 26 breakfasts within one hour is having everything to hand. I always said that breakfast at home is one of the trickiest meals to put

together, what with all the grilling, frying and poaching to take care of.

At Tyddyn Llan I bake my vine tomatoes with a splash of olive oil, black pepper and Maldon salt, and fry quarter brown cap mushrooms in olive oil and butter. I slowly fry the sausages, at first, to give them a golden colour – and, by the way, never prick the sausages as that lets all the goodness out – then pop them into a low oven for 10 minutes. My sausages are big and fat! The fried bread is cooked in sunflower oil, as bacon fat would not go down too well with our vegetarian customers, while the black pudding is cut into small discs and fried at the last minute, so all that remains is to grill the bacon and cook the eggs.

My tip for the eggs is use free range and make sure they are as fresh as possible. If they feel heavy they should be fresh and just plop out of their shells. Do not be mean with the oil,

and use plenty of water for the poached eggs, but no salt and only a dash of vinegar – and use wine vinegar. As for scrambled, if the eggs are free range the colour will be a beautifully bright colour (my step Dad always thought that I used food colouring). I don't put too much butter in the pan, and leave a little of the whisked egg in the bowl. I cook over a low heat and take it off just before it's ready, add the bit left in the bowl, stirring off the heat. This way you will get the perfect scrambled egg to go with some thinly sliced smoked salmon.

Apart from the cooked breakfast we also offer some boiled Carmarthen ham with cheese, and an assortment of salamis and cured meats. Then there's a buffet table loaded with local organic yoghurt, freshly squeezed juices, segments of pink grapefruit and bowls of seasonal fruits.

Compôte of fruits

A compôte of fruit is a very versatile dish served as a dessert during darker months with a dollop of rich homemade ice cream, or for breakfast with a covering of natural organic yoghurt. Whichever meal you wish to serve it as, it is a very satisfying way to either start the day or finish a meal.

Compôte means stewed, but the way I put it together it is merely poached for a few minutes, then left to stand in the poaching liquor for hours or days as it only gets better with time. One poached fruit that really appreciates standing in its juices is pears cooked in red wine. Take eight large pears – they must be ripe, though, so buy them a few days ahead. I always feel that pears dictate to you when they are to be cooked as one day they can still be as hard as golf balls, then the next day you check them and they must be cooked, because if you don't they are past it as quickly as they had ripened. Into a saucepan pour a bottle of red wine and add 150g of sugar, four whole cloves, two black peppercorns, one vanilla pod, one cinnamon stick, three strips of orange peel without the pith, and a few slices of crystallized ginger. Bring to the boil and add the pears, peeled and cored. Lower the heat and poach for about five minutes until soft to the touch. Leave in the juice for about a week and eat them with ice cream. They will look and taste wonderful.

These days supermarkets are very good at selling a wide selection of semi-dried fruits. At the moment I am addicted to strips of dried mango. But to make a good compôte, look for semi-dried figs and apricots. The best ones come from Turkey and Morocco – I was amazed at the stalls selling them in Marrakech, all stacked so high and so proud. But for prunes I would go for the famous ones from the south west of France. In a town called Agen, in the centre of Armagnac making area, they come already pitted and are first class; armagnac and prune make a perfect marriage.

For a breakfast compote simply put the figs and apricots into a pan, half cover with orange juice and a few drops of lemon juice. Then cover them with water, as much brown sugar as you wish, a few cinnamon sticks and a couple of Earl Grey tea bags, bring to the boil, add the prunes and take off the heat. Cover with a lid and leave to cool down and there you have a healthy option ready, for days, to get you going in more ways than one!

On the subject of poaching fruit, figs are very popular at the restaurant when cooked in orange juice and served with lemon sorbet. They make a refreshing end to the meal and are so easy to cook and serve. Just look out for large ripe figs when next shopping.

Poached figs in orange juice

Ingredients

250ml fresh orange juice
125ml lemon juice
250g caster sugar
150ml white wine
100ml brandy
10 mint leaves
8 large ripe figs

Serves 4

1 Put all the ingredients in a saucepan except the figs, bring to the boil then lower the heat and skim off any scum that will rise to the surface.

2 Add the figs, cover with a sheet of grease proof paper and gently poach on a very low heat for 5 minutes, leave to cool.

3 Serve the figs sliced in half with the juice and a scoop of lemon sorbet.

Compôte of autumn fruits

Ingredients

Juice of one lemon and one orange
500ml red wine
450g caster sugar
1 vanilla pod
1 bay leaf
1 cinnamon stick
12 peppercorns
2 Earl Grey teabags
12 prunes
12 semi dried apricots
4 large fresh figs
2 small pears

Serves 4

1 Put all the ingredients other than the fruit into a saucepan and simmer for 20 minutes to infuse all the flavourings.

2 Strain into a clean pan, peel and core the pears and place in the poaching liquid with the apricots and simmer for 5 minutes. Add figs and prunes and simmer for a further 2 to 3 minutes, cover with a sheet of greaseproof paper and leave to cool. Cinnamon ice cream goes particularly well with these flavours.

Laverbread

Apart from the traditional way of serving it with bacon and cockles, it's great to go in a creamy sauce with fish, in tarts and quiches with leeks or bacon. At Tyddyn Llan we serve it in small tarts as canapés and at breakfast we offer laverbread in an overcoat with a choice of smoked salmon or crispy bacon. This dish makes a great supper snack or if you make smaller portions, a fine starter.

Laverbread in an overcoat

Ingredients

200g laverbread
A dash of tarragon vinegar
4 slices of good country style bread
75g Welsh salted butter
8 free range eggs
100ml double cream
8 slices of smoked salmon
or 8 slices of streaky bacon
Salt and pepper

Serves 4

1 Heat the laverbread in a small saucepan with a dash of tarragon vinegar and keep warm.

2 Grill the bacon if using until crispy.

3 Break the eggs into a bowl, add the cream and mix well, season with salt and pepper.

4 Melt 50g of butter, add the eggs and over a low heat gently scramble. I find it best to turn off the heat halfway through as the heat in the pan is enough to finish the cooking process. While the eggs are cooking toast the bread.

5 To assemble; butter the toast, divide the laverbread on top of the toast, gently cover with the lightly scrambled eggs and top with either the salmon or bacon.

Canapés

Canapés may seem fancy but in fact they are practical. At Tyddyn Llan we serve a selection of canapés with drinks to assuage the pangs of hunger while the guests read the menu. They are also very good for an informal drinks party, just left on trays for your guests to pick at. The word canapé means sofa in French and conjures up an unappealing image of cold toast cut up into small pieces and covered with mean amounts of smoked salmon. But canapés should be robustly flavoured to compete with a flute of Champagne or the power of a martini cocktail.

These days you could go to an upmarket supermarket and buy a huge range of canapés, open the packets, pop them in the oven then onto to trays and serve, but your guests might have a good idea where they came from and it will cost you a fortune. So try making them yourself, it will be time consuming but very rewarding. All the work can be done a day or two in advance, and if you fancy homemade canapés while you sip your mulled wine before Christmas lunch it will only take 10 minutes to put together.

There are lots of interesting canapés to make without cold toast: goujons of fish with a Thai dip, tiny fish cakes, wonton skins filled with ricotta cheese, chopped salami and Parmesan deep fried, cubes of ripe melon wrapped with Carmarthen ham and popped onto a cocktail stick, mini scotch eggs using quail eggs, little tarts using ready made cases filled with anything you fancy – we use laverbread and leeks mixed with an egg and egg yolk, about 200ml of milk and cream and a spoonful of Parmesan, or a skewer of cherry tomatoes, feta cheese and tapenade. Even leftover risotto, rolled into small balls with a coating of breadcrumbs, make tasty little bites. One tip, try to use Panko breadcrumbs, coat your cakes or croquettes on the day you are going to fry them and use an electric deep fat fryer.

If you are holding a drinks party over the festive period, try to offer six to eight different nibbles, which can, if necessary, be supplemented with crisps, nuts and olives. I would offer two to three pieces of each canapé to the guests but it's up to you. The more you make the more they will disappear!

Parmesan biscuits

Ingredients

335g flour
300g Parmesan, grated
300g unsalted butter
A pinch of cayenne pepper
2 tablespoons of water
1 egg, beaten
50g sesame seeds

Makes 150

1 Put the flour, Parmesan and butter cut up into small pieces into a food processor and whiz until it resembles fine crumbs.

2 Add the water and pepper and work to a dough, roll out into a cylinder. Wrap in cling film and refrigerate overnight; they will keep up to a week in the fridge.

3 Brush the cylinder with beaten egg and roll in the sesame seeds. Chill until needed.

4 Cut the cylinder into 5mm slices and bake on a tray for 8 minutes at 180°C.

5 Cool and serve.

Smoked salmon roulade

Ingredients

400g smoked salmon sliced
100g cream cheese
A little chopped dill
Juice of half a lemon

Makes 20 pieces

1 Place a sheet of cling film on a clean work surface and lay onto it two to three slices of the salmon side by side, trim the salmon so that it's about 3cm wide, repeat with another sheet of cling film.

2 Put all the trimmings into a food processor with the cream cheese and purée to a smooth paste, add the lemon juice and dill, mix well and check the seasoning.

3 Put into a piping bag with a plain nozzle and pipe onto the salmon in a big line.

4 Holding the cling film roll up and refrigerate until needed. To serve slice into 1 cm pieces and remove the cling film.

Ham croquets

Ingredients

400ml milk with 1 bay leaf, a sprig of thyme,
    and parsley
75g flour
50g butter
120g Parma or Carmarthen ham, chopped small
Flour, egg wash and breadcrumbs to coat

Makes 40 pieces

1 Infuse the milk with the herbs and leave for
20 minutes. Strain into a jug.

2 Melt the butter in a clean saucepan and add
the flour, then slowly add the milk a little at
the time. It will look like a very thick white
sauce. Cook for 10 minutes very slowly. Add
the chopped ham.

3 Oil a tray and put the mixture into the tray.
Leave to cool.

4 The day you are going to serve, tip the mix
onto a board and cut into bite size pieces,
then coat with flour then egg and finally
breadcrumbs, put into the fridge for a few
hours.

5 To serve, heat a deep fryer to 190°C and fry
until golden brown.

Leek and laverbread tart

Ingredients

4 leeks, washed and finely chopped
50g butter
200g laverbread
3 egg yolks
1 whole egg
200ml double cream
200ml milk
100g Welsh cheddar, finely grated
1 shortcrust pastry case
Salt and pepper

Serves 4

1 Bake the pastry case blind for 20 minutes
at 180°C.

2 Cook the leeks in butter until soft and mix
with the laverbread.

3 Mix the egg and yolks with the cream and
milk add to the leeks and laverbread and mix
well, season with salt and pepper.

4 Pour into the cooked pastry case, top with
the cheese and bake at 150°C for about 30
minutes until just set. Serve warm with a
crisp salad.

Shortcrust pastry

Ingredients

250g plain flour
160g unsalted butter
1 whole egg
1 tablespoon of milk
Pinch of salt

1 Mix all the dry ingredients in a food
processor or large bowl, add the milk and egg
and mix well, wrap in cling film and leave to
rest in a fridge for 1 hour before rolling into a
tart case.

Cheese

I feel that if you are going to have a dinner party you must include a cheese course for many reasons, not the least being that as the host it's the time you can sit down and relax. I would always serve the cheese before the pudding because I do not like the taste buds going from savoury to sweet and back to savoury, and it's a good excuse to finish off the red wine or, better still, open another bottle. I find port too sweet but it's all a matter of taste as Susan would happily have a glass of port or three.

Today there is an enormous variety of cheeses to choose from, many of which come from the UK. When I started out in the business some 30 years ago, British cheese consisted only of Cheddar, Caerphilly and Stilton and cheap horrid plastic cheese. In fact I do not remember my mum ever having cheese in the house except at Christmas. When I started work there was a cheese board with about a dozen different cheeses on and I was told that France could offer a different cheese for every day of the year. These days the British have caught up and we have a great selection to offer.

At Tyddyn Llan we buy our cheese from Neal's Yard Dairy. They are the best cheese suppliers in this country. You should visit them in Covent Garden in London, the shop is fantastic. But Chester also has a great cheese shop, called The Cheese Shop, on Northgate Street, and Blas ar Fwyd in Llanrwst stock a good range of cheese. The problem with cheese is that it has to be ripe, which is where Neal's Yard gets it right. Also the cheese has to be served at room temperature. If it's straight from the fridge it's not worth eating. You have to look after cheese and wrap it in waxed paper, as cling firm is only suitable for hard cheese.

So let's blow the trumpet for Welsh cheese.

Cheese should be pure and natural, so let's forget the smoked and flavoured ones with chilli, ginger and other silly ideas. My ideal Welsh cheese board would be a Pant Mawr Preseli, which is a soft and creamy cow's milk with its natural rind; Perl Wen, a Brie style cheese with a very clean flavour; Caerphilly from Gorwydd, a real farmhouse unpasteurised Caerphilly with a natural dark rind; Llanboidy Cheddar from a rare breed Red Poll herd, which is a firm, medium mature with a deep flavour; Celtic Promise, which is a true artisan unpasteurised washed rind with full rich farmyard flavours and smells; and, for blue, there are two choices: the Perl Las, which is a lively mature flavour of creamy blue or the Gorau Glas from Anglesey, which is a fantastic cheese but the price is frightening.

I love cheese in cooking; the Parmesan that goes into a risotto or the pile of Cheddar that tops some toast for a midnight snack attack, but a good Welsh rarebit, Glamorgan sausage or cheese beignets make great canapés or starters.

Glamorgan sausages

Ingredients

500g Caerphilly cheese
¼ of a white fresh loaf of bread
2 tablespoons of chopped chives
1 teaspoon of chopped thyme
2 tablespoons of chopped parsley
1 tablespoon of mustard powder
Salt and pepper
1 teaspoon of beaten egg
Plain flour
2 to 3 beaten eggs
Stale breadcrumbs for coating

Makes about 60

1 Remove the crusts from the bread and make into breadcrumbs using a food processor.

2 Grate the cheese into a large mixing bowl, add the breadcrumbs and all the other ingredients and mix very well.

3 Roll into a cylinder shape, depending what you are going to use the sausages for; for canapés roll thinly or as a starter or main course roll to the thickness of a normal sausage.

4 Cut the sausages to the length you require and put into the flour, then the beaten egg and finally breadcrumbs. It is best to do the egg and breadcrumbs twice.

5 Shallow fry or deep fry until golden brown. This recipe makes quite a large quantity as the sausages don't work well in small batches.

Welsh rarebit

Ingredients

700g mature Cheddar

150ml milk

25g plain flour

50g fresh white breadcrumbs

1 tablespoon of English mustard powder

2 shakes of Worcestershire sauce

Salt and pepper

2 eggs

2 egg yolks

1 Put the milk and cheese in a saucepan and slowly melt the cheese but do not boil.

2 Add the flour, breadcrumbs and mustard and cook for a few minutes stirring all the time until the mixture comes away from the side of the pan and forms a ball shape. Add the Worcestershire sauce, salt and pepper. Leave to cool covered with cling film.

3 When cool put the mix in a food processor and add the eggs, to form a smooth paste. Chill for a few hours. The mix has many uses simply grilled on crunchy toast or topped on a piece of smoked haddock. It also freezes very well – divide into four and freeze three for later use.

Chocolate truffles

Ingredients

660g chocolate, roughly chopped
200g double cream at room temperature
300g unsalted butter
50ml rum (optional)
300g of extra chocolate for coating

Makes about 30

1 Melt the chocolate and butter in a bowl over a saucepan of hot water.

2 Bring the cream to boil for a few seconds and take off the heat and slightly cool, mix into the melted chocolate and butter.

3 Add the rum if using and continue to mix until smooth and shiny.

4 Pour into a tray and leave to set.

5 Use a large melon baller (Parisian scoop) to form balls of the mixture, ball out on to a tray lined with greaseproof paper and leave to set in a refrigerator.

6 Melt the extra chocolate in the same way, with a cocktail stick or fork quickly dip the truffles in the chocolate and place back onto the tray. You can also at this stage roll them in some top quality cocoa powder.

Fudge

I don't do fancy petit fours. They are just not me. To me, a good chocolate truffle and a square of fudge is enough to go with the coffee at the end of a meal, although this was not always the case. I remember many lunches out with fellow chefs and, in particular, at the Waterside Inn at Bray where we would easily devour all the beautiful and delicious petit fours before asking for seconds.

This fudge recipe came from a great chef and friend, big Jeremy, who did two stints in Hilaire's kitchen as my second. (At one point he also worked for the now famous television chef Nick Nairn, where I believe the recipe originated.) In Scotland they call it Tablet. There is a wonderful lady from San Francisco who stays with us at Tyddyn Llan every year; she loves this stuff and takes a tin of it back to the States.

Tablet fudge

Ingredients

1 tin of condensed milk
250g butter
1 kg sugar
250ml still mineral water
100g white chocolate

1 Put all the ingredients into a large saucepan, Stir to break down the sugar, put onto a medium heat and stir from time to time to make sure that it's not sticking. Bring to the boil and boil for about 40 minutes until thick, stirring constantly at this stage. Once the mix is thick remove from the heat and add the chocolate. Be very careful as it is very hot.

2 Pour into the tray and when it's cool enough to cut, cut into bite size squares.

shortbread

Ingredients

500g plain flour
250g butter
125g caster sugar
Pinch of salt

Makes about 30 pieces

1 Cream the butter and sugar together.

2 Add the flour and salt and work to a dough.

3 Grease a shallow tray and put the mixture into the tray.

4 Bake in the oven at 150°C for 50 minutes.

5 Remove from the oven and generously sprinkle with caster sugar.

6 Before it cools down cut into shortbread fingers.

Biscotti

Ingredients

420g plain flour
200g caster sugar
75g whole blanched almonds
50g flaked almonds
2 tablespoons of polenta
1½ teaspoons of baking powder
A pinch of salt
80g unsalted butter
2 whole eggs
1 tablespoon of Pernod
1 egg white, lightly beaten
1 extra tablespoon of caster sugar.

1 Preheat the oven to 175°C.

2 Combine the flour, sugar, polenta, baking powder, and salt into a bowl of a mixing machine, using the paddle attachment on a low speed mix together.

3 Add the butter, mix well then add the whole eggs, vanilla and Pernod until soft dough is formed.

4 Divide the dough into four logs about 25cm long, place onto a baking tray lined with parchment paper, brush the logs with the egg white and sprinkle with the extra tablespoon of sugar.

5 Bake for 30 minutes until golden brown, firm and pliable. Leave on the tray to cool.

6 Cut using a serrated knife about ½ cm thick. Lay the slices out onto a tray, lower the oven temperature to 150°C and bake for 10 to 12 minutes.

7 Cool and store in an airtight container.

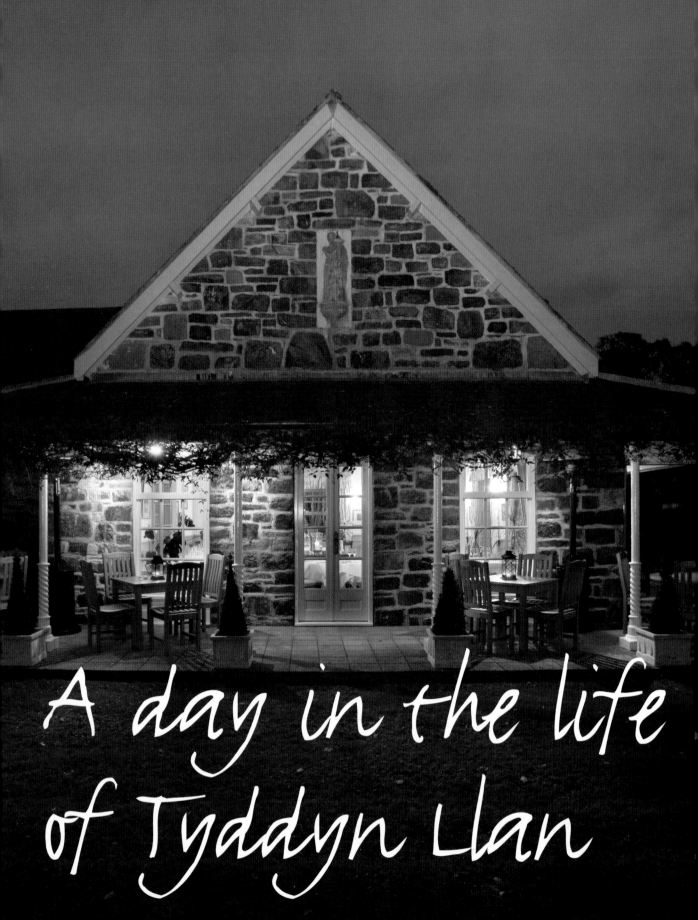

A day in the life of Tyddyn Llan

One of the delights of starting my day at Tyddyn Llan is not having to be squashed on the Tube, trying to hail a cab or dodging the traffic on my bicycle in the hope of getting to work as early as possible. I just walk 20 paces and that's it, I am in the kitchen. There's always a great feel to stepping into the kitchen first thing in the morning. Everything is shining and in its right place. It looks so clean and tidy, and on a early spring or summer morning with the sun shining through the windows, it makes a great start to the day.

I am always the first in the kitchen, normally just before eight, unless it's the shooting season when breakfast may be required as early as 7am. I enjoy breakfast. The juices are all freshly prepared, segments of grapefruits and compôte are all laid out on a buffet table, and once all the preparations are ready, it's just a waiting game. As we believe guests are here to relax, we serve breakfast until well after 10am. While waiting, it gives me the opportunity to check all the fridges, making sure that everything is in order. It's also time to put yesterday's stocks on to reduce to a glacé, or a duck sauce to be reduced to the right consistency. And duck confit that has been absorbing the salt, herbs and aromas overnight needs to be slowly cooked in duck fat in the oven. I'll also chase and place any orders.

Breakfast

By 8am the ladies who serve breakfast should hopefully have arrived and it's time for the first of the tea and coffee trays to be taken up to the rooms for a gentle morning call. Geraint should then turn up with the newspapers and eggs – I am usually down to my last dozen – fresh yoghurt is handed over to Megan, and it goes straight out to the buffet table.

Gradually breakfast picks up pace and the orders are duly prepared. Without a crystal ball you can never judge if you have made enough porridge, grilled too many sausages or have enough haddock to poach. Some days it's so popular, other days no one wants it. Just before 10am, as the last residents stroll into the dining room, the chefs who help me in the preparation start to arrive. While breakfast has been served the housekeepers have been tidying the lounges, cleaning the back of house, laying the fire, and cleaning the office before Carol arrives at 9am to begin checking out any guests who are leaving that day. The laundry, towels, dressing gowns and staff uniforms also all need to be washed and ready.

Deliveries

Keltic might just phone – I don't really want to take the call as it means they haven't landed big enough scallops, or the langoustine haven't been caught – but sometimes the news isn't so bad; it may be that the courier company will be late with the delivery. This isn't the

end of the world as the crabs and lobster will arrive soon so there's plenty to get on with. When the glacé and duck sauce have reached the right consistency, they are strained into plastic containers, and this leaves room on the stove to make fresh veal and chicken stocks. The veal bones have been in the oven for half an hour or more by then, as Paul, the delivery man for the butcher, will have been by 9am. Likewise the chicken bones will have been under running water ready to go on as soon as breakfast is finished.

Lunch

We only serve lunch on Fridays, Saturdays and Sundays. Sunday is the busiest, and a job I like to have under my belt before breakfast that day is the Yorkshire pudding mix, so it has enough time to stand.

Kasia, one of the housekeepers who looks after me like a second wife, will supply me with my first pot of Earl Grey as soon as she can and, by the end of breakfast, a large mug of Cleanse tea will also come my way. She knows how to look after someone. On the weekend, Susan will be through early to prepare the bills, as Carol is a Monday to Friday girl, and on Saturdays you will always hear *The Sound of the Sixties* playing on the computer while she waits for the first check out.

Bread

Bread is one of the first jobs for the pastry department. We make three to four types a day, plus breadsticks. On a Sunday it can become quite a job jostling for oven space with Yorkshires, roasties and a sirloin all happily cooking away, and canapés have to be baked as well.

Jobs on the list

Everyone prepares the jobs on the list: smoked salmon terrine, pumpkin soup, a fresh tray of shortbread, chips to be cut, potato pancake mix, spinach to be picked. When the delivery from Wild Harvest arrives, there should be an array of mushrooms to be cleaned. James will have two ice creams and a sorbet to churn in our small ice cream machine, the timers are ringing, the brulées are ready and that big saucepan of confit needs lifting out of the oven. Once the Wild Harvest delivery has been checked, and everything is in order, I have a terrine of foie gras to make and the pigeons need to be prepared. Marcin loves his little birds. Meanwhile all through the morning the piles of washing up will have been disappearing with the help of my Polish porters.

At 12.15pm on a Sunday people will start to approach down the drive but we are not ready. Canapés are still being panned, and the shallots for the risotto still need to be chopped, but we will be ready by 12.45pm – the time of the first booking. The Yorkshires are rising perfectly and we are ready to roll; trays of canapés are ready to be served once called. The first order comes in: two salmon, one crab, one mozzarella, three beef – two pink, one well done – one rabbit.

By 1.20pm it feels like a coach has pulled up. There's a queue at the front door and the car park is full with cars parked on the main road. Bloody Marys are flying off the bar and there are calls for more Champagne. As the chambermaids walk into the kitchen, adding to the piles of washing up with the used morning tea trays, the kitchen looks in organised chaos. Table 10 mains away; table 18 starters away; more bread for table one, the large family party of 12...

By two o'clock about 30 main courses have been served. Matthew is looking for bin number 128 on the list, while dessert checks start to arrive on James's side of the kitchen. Martin is sent over to help while Siôn and I concentrate on getting the last few tables food ready. Susan's desperately looking for two more bottles of chilled pink Champagne, as residents are now asking to sit on deckchairs on the lawn in the sunshine sipping Champagne. If only! The reception bell is ringing; there are people to check in, customers waiting to pay the bill; while room 11 and 12 have ordered four full afternoon teas.

Where is Susan? Talking to the customers; making the customer feel special. It's what she does best. But I need to speak to her. "Offer table eight a digestif. They are regulars and it's his birthday".

By 3.00pm the last mains have gone, and the last of the desserts have been sent out. Coffee is being served around the pond on the terrace and in the lounges. People are everywhere and the dining room starts to become quiet. The head waiter goes off for his break, and the kitchen serve the remaining beef and lamb to the staff to give them the energy to continue, as the dining room needs cleaning and setting up for the evening service. Megan goes around the lounges and puffs up the cushions and makes them look fresh, while the kitchen staff continue with the endless prep work to be ready for dinner at 7pm.

By 4.30pm the chefs take a break. They will be back at six. While the chambermaids check all the rooms, the waiters clear the final coffee cups and wine glasses. By 6pm the whole place is calm. Two couples are quietly reading the newspapers, while the restaurant is set to go for part three. Candles are lit, menus printed and the seating plan has had the final adjustments made. The check-in daily room sheet is waiting for the last room to arrive before telephoning the local shop with the newspaper order.

Evening service

The kitchen slowly gears up for the evening service. Chips are blanching, while vegetables are cooked off, ready to be flash-heated during service. The phone rings. It's room 10: "Please can we order a bottle of 181 and have it decanted. We'll be down at eight for dinner". I arrange my fridge and bench while being handed spoons, whisks and spatulas in a small bucket of hot water ready at arm's reach. Everything is in place. We are ready. Czarek hands me a large espresso and we await the call of canapés.

At 7pm guests are arriving. There are 38 booked, but all before 8.30pm, so it's going to be a fast one. Susan walks through the kitchen, looking glamorous, after just finishing her nightly briefing with the waiting staff. Wait for it... she's hungry. "Paying customers come first", I say, handing over a cup of watercress soup to keep her hunger pains at bay. The first canapés have gone as I whisk butter into a beurre blanc reduction, and Siôn checks the fondants and finishes off a fresh batch of mashed potato. The first check is on. It's a shopping list: one crab, one scallops, one terrine of foie gras, one Imam Bayildi, one red mullet, one lobster, then one lamb, one bass, one duck, one rabbit, two steaks – one rare, one medium no pepper and sauce on the side. Canapés for three, but one's a veggie. Is the vegetarian menu printed? Soup and bread for two. Is table 10 sat yet? Order on two tasting menus, starters table six.

A day in the life

It's 7.30pm and the heat in the kitchen is rising. Matt is grating fresh horseradish for Bloody Marys, more ice is needed for the bar, while Susan's juggling three bottles of different white wine for table 16. Main course table three: scallops on tasting menu. Check on: two soup, two scallops, two lamb. Great! An easy order. Soup and bread table 14.

It's 8pm and one of the housekeepers is back to do turndown service. She checks if all rooms are down, and off she goes to perform her task. Susan answers the telephone, "Good evening, Tyddyn Llan, please can you hold?" Check on: two tasting menu. "Hello, how can I help you?"

"Teaspoons, please. Change the spoon water. Where's the spatula I asked for? Mains away table three. Come on, desserts are waiting over there. Two veg, two fries. Siôn, please. Main courses away please. Tea strainers now!" Meanwhile the washing up is piling up at both sides as all the plates and cutlery are brought back to the kitchen. Daniela does not help by bringing more dirty glasses down from the rooms, but help's at hand as she has now finished turndown and so helps with the washing up.

"Table 10 wants to know if you can go out to speak to them. They want the recipe for the aubergine purée." "No, but I'll print one off for you." Desserts away, mains on tasting menu. "Daryl, do you know what the cheeses are tonight?" "Wigmore, Waterloo, Golden Cross, Stitchling, Double Gloucester, Keen's Cheddar, Millens and Caerphilly." "Excellent. Away, please." The last mains are gone. "What's for staff tonight?" Chilli con Carne. The fussy one doesn't like that. Give him some of Joe's burgers and there's that overcooked duck breast and some lamb on the resting tray.

Fridges are emptied, trays changed and all containers cling filmed, while James prepares the final couple of dessert checks. "How long for the chocolate trio?" "Table five, tasting menu, want a 20-minute break before dessert." Benches are cleaned down and the cooker scrubbed clean. Waiters are polishing glasses, serving coffee. "We need more fudge tomorrow. We are a bit low, okay?" "Have table two been offered digestifs with the coffee?" "Section three in the lounge wants more coffee and please, Bryan, will you come and speak to Mr and Mrs Owen? They are big regulars and have some Spanish friends with them, pleads Susan. "Okay. When they are in the bar."

The sinks are now looking a lot better, just a few cups and two saucepans. Staff meal, all plated and ready to go. Staff drinks all round and a glass of white wine for me. While the restaurant is cleared down and set up according to the plan, coffee and brandies are taken in the lounges, and the whole place has a certain hush, with the twinkling of glass and the murmur of conversation.

I sit in front of the computer with lists to make for tomorrow's prep and orders to be placed on answer machines. I'll adjust the menu as there's no crab left, but langoustines are coming tomorrow. Breakfast is all laid up and the trays for morning tea are set up. There are just a few glasses to polish, and there's one couple left in the lounge, but they seem ready for bed. "Susan, are you still hungry? Burgers and Pain chilli sauce alright?" It's midnight snack attack time. The kitchen floor has been washed, the fridge temperatures checked and the fans turned off. As I lock the office door I think, "What did I record on TV tonight?"

suppliers

Many suppliers provided me with their great products for many years in London, so it came as a blessing when we first opened at Tyddyn Llan that they would all still be able to supply me in deepest North Wales.

Wild Harvest, based in London, are great for wild mushrooms, exotic baby vegetables, truffles and a host of other things that are hard to get in Wales, ingredients such as lentille du Puy, Carnaroli risotto rice and 70 per cent chocolate. I have used them since their very early days when it was just two lads driving around London restaurants selling their goods. They also do me a great service by buying French spinach, artichokes and iron bar pumpkins from the London market. With their supplies they help me to put together an interesting menu.

There are chickens and there are Label Anglais Chickens. I was one of the first customers of the Farmyard Chicken Company which is based at Temple Farm near Harlow in Essex. Their chickens are the best that you can get in this country – as good if not better than the French poulet de Bresse with all its stickers – and the reason is that they do not use any shortcuts or modern methods in the way they raise their chickens. They started off with a cross of two old British breeds, Red Cornish and White Rock, which because of their heritage are well-suited to our climate and thrive in their free range pastures. At Temple Farm their breeding methods allow for a much slower growth to full maturity. Much more time spent scratching around the fields and hedgerows helps to develop a fuller, more satisfying flavour in the meat. To me there is no better comfort food than a roast chicken dinner using a Label Anglais chicken. The taste and flavour will be like no other chicken dinner you have had before.

If I were a chef in a big organisation where gross profit were an issue I don't think I would last that long. I can still remember the heartache, back in the very early days of Hilaire, of trying to achieve a respectable and not unreasonable gross profit of 65 per cent for Kenny Brooks who then owned it. These days companies would be expecting more in the region of 75 per cent, so giving away titbits of salted almonds, the finest green and black olives, as well as a plate of canapés, would defiantly be a big no-no. At Tyddyn Llan Susan gives me enough grief as it is, so using companies like the Fresh Olive Company and Brindisa for this would be out. But their other products are also excellent. They both have a great range of olive oils from France, Italy and Spain; specialised vinegars; the finest anchovies and capers; Juión del Barco (butter beans); Garbanzo Pedrosillano (chick peas); a charcuterie and fine range of products such as honey, mustards, harissa and a tinned tuna that makes the best tuna mayo sandwiches.

Both companies supply the best food shops and department stores in the country so that you can try these products yourself.

When we were trying to raise the capital to buy Tyddyn Llan, Susan and I would work for the True Taste of Wales, a part of the Welsh Assembly that rises the profile of Welsh food, doing cookery demonstrations and promoting Welsh products. The cheeses were amazing, all perfect and ripe and a match for any other British and continental cheese. The plan, once we were open at Tyddyn Llan, was that we would offer only Welsh cheese, which went well for the first year or so as long as we could get the cheeses ripe or ripen them up ourselves. But the choice can be a little limited, especially as I do not like the flavoured cheeses of which they tend to make far too many. So to complement our Welsh selection I contacted Neal's Yard Dairy to add a range of their cheeses. Also, for a midnight snack, nothing beats loads of grated Keen's cheddar on a door stop of bread, toasted to a golden brown. As we were getting busier, the amount of Parmesan we were using was increasing and Neal's Yard have an excellent one. I always buy what

the team at Neal's Yard recommend as their knowledge of cheese is second to none.

A delicacy which I often like to have on the menu is smoked eel, and just by chance I came across Brown and Forrest, a smokery based in Somerset that had been in business for over 20 years, and their eel was top quality. They offer a range of smoked goods which is all available via mail order.

Then there are two local gentlemen who also help me with my supplies. Firstly, Geraint the milkman who supplies me with milk, and cream, and eggs, from local farms, although he would never divulge which one. The yolks of the eggs are a bright yellow, which gives our ice cream a deep rich colour. I'm sure I stress Geraint out during our busiest periods when I want more eggs and he reckons the chicken are not laying! He also acts as our paper boy, collecting them from the village shop and bringing them at the crack of dawn, especially during the shooting season.

Ken, who lives in the historic town of Harlech, grows the most wonderful salad leaves, weather permitting. He brings them on the bus which must take a long time, and it's not as though he does not drive. During the spring and summer, Ken also keeps our vegetable garden in order, which hosts an aromatic array of herbs that get quickly used up in the kitchen.

Laverbread

Laverbread or bara lawr, the most Welsh of all the ingredients we use, is picked and cooked on the Gower coast by Selwyn's of Penclawdd. It's a great product, especially during the summer months when it has a much thicker texture.

You can also buy it in tins and a very good one is the Drangway brand. Its dark, smooth appearance makes it distinctive. Traditionally it is boiled for hours to render it to a thick purée. It is available in the markets and fishmongers of south Wales.

Best of all, just go along to the beach and pick it yourself, around the Gower coast on the beaches of Langland, Caswell and Rhossili. Thanks to my good friend Colin Pressdee, we have also discovered it growing on beaches on the Llŷn Peninsula. It's great fun to pick on a fine day. Susan and I get carried away and end up with loads of the stuff. You just get that sense of excitement when you find another pile on the rocks and you just keep going, forgetting all sense of the time. It's so addictive, so you need to be careful of any incoming tides.

Laverbread that you pick yourself make a tasty crisp, once you have washed it a few times in clean water to remove any sand, and dried it, just coat in flour and deep fry for about 3 minutes, drain and season with salt and a little chilli powder.

Llŷn Peninsula

Our fishmonger, Alan Gregory

You would think that living a country like Wales, where a large proportion of the land is surrounded by the sea, buying fresh fish would not be a problem. If Tyddyn Llan were nearer the coast I am sure that it would be a lot easier. I rely on a man who is as passionate about fresh fish as I am. Alan Gregory, with his wife Brenda, runs a small business supplying to the best restaurants and hotels in North Wales and Cheshire. Based on the Wirral, Alan has built up an enviable reputation supplying the finest fish from the day boats off the coast of Cornwall (within 24 hours of landing); wild salmon from the River Dee and sea trout from the River Tweed; superior farmed salmon from Loch Duart (which goes into our fish cakes), where every fish is traceable; and smoked salmon from the environmentally friendly Loch Fyne company. When in season, Alan also brings asparagus, strawberries and raspberries from local farms. He is always keen to find new produce and whatever my requests are – from veal cheeks and Toulouse sausages to the finest calves liver – Alan will get it. I am probably his toughest customer but over the five years a mutual respect has grown and he knows that if the product is not perfect and spanking fresh, don't send it.

the finest fish from the day boats

Albert Rees

In Carmarthen market you will find a cured ham that can rival the illustrious air-dried hams of the Mediterranean. Chris Rees took over the family's butcher's business in 1989 from his father Albert. The family have cured hams for more than five generations. Carmarthen Ham, the oldest commercially produced air-dried ham in Britain, is sliced and eaten raw, just like Serrano in Spanish tapas bars. The ham found a market 30 years ago when a local hotelier began serving it exactly as Parma or Bayonne ham, but with a local name tag. Now chefs all over Wales use this fantastic ham.

Chris Rees prepares the hams in his small plant facing west over the Tywi Estuary. Most weeks he takes in at least 30 legs of pork to keep his curing line topped up, plus sides for bacon. After butchering and trimming, the hams are put into a deep vat and rubbed with saltpetre and his secret ingredient. He refuses to divulge this except to say it has been passed down through the generations. For each ham he uses a fist-load of the mixture and repeats the procedure every two days. This forms the crust through which the moisture in the ham will gradually evaporate. After three weeks, the hams are transferred to his drying room. A further three weeks pass, then the best are selected to mature for six months, while the other 30 per cent are sold as gammon steaks, boiling joints or cooked whole as York hams.

Despite competition from large companies and the imported market, it's great to see that a great Welsh product can be so successful. If you want to try the ham I know that it's available from Blas ar Fwyd in Llanwrst and Rees owns a stall in Carmarthen market. A canapé that we serve at Tyddyn Llan using Carmarthen ham with leeks is very simple: just clean three or four tender leeks and put them into a plastic dish. Season with salt and pepper and a dash of balsamic vinegar, cover with cling film and microwave on high until soft. Leave to cool, then lay out some sheets of cling film on a table and place slices of ham on the cling film. Put the leeks on top, then roll the ham around the leeks using the cling film. Refrigerate, then slice into half-inch pieces and serve.

the family have cured hams for more than five generations

Carmarthen ham with warm wilted greens

Ingredients

2 tablespoons of red wine vinegar

1 large shallot, peeled and finely chopped

1 clove of garlic, peeled and finely grated

A pinch of salt and pepper

4 tablespoons of olive oil

4 large handfuls of greens (about 250g),
    washed and dried, such as young spinach
    leaves, rocket, frisée or bok choy

16 very thin slices of Carmarthen ham

Serves 4

1 Mix the vinegar, olive oil, shallots and garlic together and season with salt and pepper.

2 Place this vinaigrette in a large saucepan or wok and place over a low heat.

3 Add the greens; if your pan is not big enough, do this in smaller batches, toss them continually with a pair of tongs for about 1 minute, until slightly wilted but not limp.

4 Remove from the heat, and place a small mixture of greens on each slice of ham, roll up and serve warm with a little of the dressing drizzled over the top.

Our butcher, T.J.Roberts & son

One of the main differences between cooking in Wales and in London is that customers eat a lot more meat, which is why, thankfully, I have a brilliant butcher. In London I swore by the famous Allen's of Mayfair but my local butcher in Bala is even better. Haydn, one of the four partners, is the fourth generation running the business with three other family members – his Mum, Dad and sister. It's a real family business. It was started in 1878 by Haydn's great-great-grandfather, Thomas John, who gave up his job as a mole catcher to open a butcher's shop. Back then there were six butchers in the town, but soon there was to be only one, T.J. Roberts. Their well hung, aged Welsh Black beef, is bought from local farms; the organic pigs come from Llanuwchllyn; and the lambs are bought from the Bala cattle

market for most of the year and straight from farms during the Spring. Apart from all this excellent meat, they give you the most amazing service: nothing is too much trouble, from a smile and a chat in the shop to delivering on a Sunday when you've discovered that the number of Sunday lunches has doubled and there is not enough beef to go round.

Three years ago they moved with the times and made the other half of their shop into a delicatessen which sells their homemade steak pies, hand raised pork pies and amazing faggots, together with Welsh cheese, hams and fresh fish via Alan Gregory. I only hope that the good folk of Bala know how lucky they are to have such a great butcher's shop in the town, because I know how lucky I am for them to supply me.

Our delicatessen, Blas ar Fwyd

When you run a restaurant you never need to visit a supermarket. Well, maybe sometimes for the cat food. Our dry products, along with a huge range of other things, come though a very Welsh company, Blas ar Fwyd, which is based about 30 miles away in the small town of Llanrwst. In 1988 Deiniol first established a delicatessen, which has grown into a restaurant, an outside catering company and wholesale trader to a vast area of Wales.

Through Blas ar Fwyd we buy Edwards of Conwy dry cured back bacon, black pudding and pork and leek sausages, the basics of sugar and organic flour for baking our bread, though to local Welsh honey and jellies. No product seems to be a problem for them to source from a wide range of suppliers which they import directly from the producer.

They even bake Bara Brith and Welsh cakes for us, which we serve at afternoon tea. They offer the widest range of Welsh farmhouse cheese from goats, sheep and cows that graze naturally and freely on the hills of the Welsh uplands, and even our wine list is given a helping hand from some of their wines from specialised vineyards across the world.

Our seafoods, Keltic seafare

I started using Keltic Seafare back in late 1995 when the company I was using could not get any supplies and they were able to supply me with scallops over the Christmas period. From that day I have never bought a scallop from anywhere else. They are the best in the world and I must say I have never had any problems, except for the Scottish weather. The company was set up in 1993 by Eddie Hughson with Marian and Laurence Watkins and over the years has built up an enviable reputation for its products and service. I buy their extra large king scallops, which are diver-caught off the northwest coast of Scotland, and their creel-caught langoustines, which arrive at Tyddyn Llan individually packed in tubes so they don't fight on their journey and so are alive and kicking before they hit the pot. Keltic claim that the scallops and langoustine get from the seabed to the kitchen within 18 hours and from the quality it must be true. Also, during the summer months, they offer an extra product – the cleanest and most perfect Girolles mushrooms, picked by their local pickers. They tend to make their way into many dishes at that time of the year.

extra large king scallops, diver-caught off the northwest coast

To finish

I am no pastry chef, I really admire chefs who are, it's such a creative art and takes a lot of skill, only the large kitchens can really justify to having someone dedicated just to that section, preparing all the desserts, ice creams, petit fours as well as baking the daily bread.

I do not have a sweet tooth and this does reflect in the style of desserts we make,

there may be a few exceptions such as ginger pudding. During the summer I love summer pudding or just a bowl of perfect ripe fruit, while my choice to finish off many a good meal would be a simple sorbet or ice cream.

My choice to finish off many a good meal would be a simple sorbet or ice cream.

Caramel ice cream

Ingredients

250g sugar
150ml water
2 vanilla pods, split lengthways
8 eggs
350ml milk
200ml double cream

1 Make a caramel with the sugar, water and vanilla pods, and try and take it as dark as you dare.

2 Heat the milk and cream and carefully pour over the caramel, being careful that it does not boil over.

3 Pour over the egg yolks.

4 Cook to a thick custard.

5 Cool and churn.

Vanilla ice cream

Ingredients

300ml milk
300ml double cream
2 vanilla pods
250g sugar
6 egg yolks

1 Mix the cream and milk together, cut the vanilla pods in half and scrape the seeds into the creamy milk and drop the pods in as well.

2 Heat the mixture and leave to infuse.

3 In a saucepan boil the sugar with water to 106°C (jam on a sugar thermometer) and pour over the egg yolks.

4 Add the hot infused creamy milk.

5 Leave to cool, strain and churn.

Prune and mascarpone ice cream

Ingredients

250ml double cream
250ml milk
1 split vanilla pod
250g sugar
6 egg yolks
250g mascarpone
10ml Armagnac
10 stoned and chopped prunes

1 Warm the milk, cream and vanilla.

2 Boil the sugar with a little water to 106°C and pour over the egg yolks and add the hot milk and cream.

3 When cool, strain through a sieve and mix with 250g mascarpone cheese.

4 Add 10 stoned and chopped prunes and 10ml of Armagnac.

5 Churn in the ice cream machine.

Orange sorbet

Ingredients

1 litre of orange juice
300g icing sugar

1 Mix together and churn.

Pineapple sorbet

Ingredients

1 litre of pineapple purée
350g icing sugar
150ml water
Juice of 1 orange
2 tablespoons white rum

1 Mix all the ingredients together, strain though a sieve and churn.

Chocolate

I think it would be safe to say that most people love chocolate. My wife does, and on special occasions I have sent for probably the best chocolates in the world from a shop in London's Bond Street.

When cooking with chocolate you have to use the very best quality, with at least 50 per cent solid cocoa content or, even better, look out for 60 to 70 per cent. Bitter chocolate is the ultimate cooking chocolate. There is plain chocolate; bittersweet chocolate; milk chocolate, which is no good for cooking; and white chocolate, which is not chocolate as it does not contain chocolate liquor. Shops like Blas ar Fwyd in Llanrwst will sell this finest quality of chocolates. Never use the artificial stuff that calls itself cooking chocolate. A bar of plain Bourneville will do if needs must. The chocolate cheesecake recipe was given to me over 20 years ago by the head chef of Inverlochy Castle in Scotland when it was regarded as one of the finest restaurants in the country.

Chocolate cheesecake

Ingredients

150g chocolate
250g full fat cream cheese
125g sugar
2 large eggs, separated
150ml double cream
1 leaf of gelatine or 5g of powdered
    gelatine
150g chocolate digestive biscuits
10g unsalted butter

Serves 8

1 Grind the biscuits in a food processor, melt the butter, add the biscuits and stir until hot, put into a 20cm spring release cake tin and press down.

2 Melt the chocolate in a bowl over a saucepan of warm water.

3 Melt the gelatine in a tablespoon of hot water.

4 In a clean food processor bowl, put the cream cheese, sugar and egg yolks.

5 Whip the cream to a soft peak and in a separate bowl whip the egg whites to a soft peak.

6 Add the melted chocolate and gelatine to the cream cheese mixture and mix together, pour into a large clean bowl.

7 Gently fold in the cream followed by the egg whites, when completely mixed together pour into the cake tin, leave to set in a refrigerator over night.

8 Serve with grated chocolate on top. Sorry, it's a lot of bowls and washing up, but it will be worth it!

Chocolate pithiviers

Ingredients

1 mix of pastry cream (see page 165)
1 packet of puff pastry
Beaten egg to glaze
Icing sugar for dusting

For the chocolate filling

100g unsalted butter
100g caster sugar
2 small eggs
100g ground almonds
50g cocoa powder
1 teaspoon dark rum
100g plain bitter chocolate, chopped into
   tiny pieces

Serves 4

1 For the filling, cream the butter and sugar together until light and fluffy, add the eggs one by one and beat again, add the almonds, cocoa powder, beat again, add the rum and pastry cream and finally stir in the chopped chocolate, chill.

2 Roll out the pastry into 10cm squares and 15cm squares. Place the smaller squares onto a floured surface and using an ice cream scoop place a ball of the chilled mix in the centre. Brush with beaten egg and put the large squares on top, press down and around firmly. Using a 10cm round pastry cutter cut the filled squares into rounds, press the edges with a fork to seal, chill.

3 Pre heat the oven to 200°C, brush the pasties with egg and bake on a tray using bakewell paper for 15 to 18 minutes until the pastry is golden, puffed, shiny and crisp. Remove and dust with icing sugar, serve with crème fraiche or thick cream.

Chocolate pithiviers

Chocolate pithiviers, or pasty as I always call it, was on the menu at Hilaire restaurant in London when I took over as chef from Simon Hopkinson some 20 years ago. Simon got the idea from a top restaurant in France where the chef refused to give him the recipe, so he worked this one out himself, and it has been on my menus ever since. Crème Fraiche goes wonderfully with this dessert and I recommend the supermarket with the *Finest* range, it is as good as you will get from France.

Crème brulée

I must have been making Crème Brulée for over 25 years using different amounts of ingredients and methods of cooking. Over the years it has always been on a menu of mine in different versions and flavours and it has always been one of the most popular desserts.

Traditionally it was always served in a large dish. Its English name, Burnt Cream, is credited to Trinity College, Cambridge, and has carried the name Trinity Burnt Cream ever since. For practical reasons, these days it's served in individual pots, but I am unsure when we all started calling it Crème Brulée.

Crème Brulée has so few ingredients that it demands the best cream and free range eggs. Jersey cream, untouched by methods of pasteurisation, would be fantastic, but these days it's hard to find an untreated pot of gorgeous yellow cream. We used to buy it from Bower Farm but transport problems arose. If you are in Abergavenny or Raglan look out for this cream; buy a punnet of strawberries and treat yourself.

When there are lots of fresh soft fruits around, put some in the bottom of the dish before you pour in the custard. My preference would be whimberries, which are found growing wild on the moors. Very Welsh.

Trinity burnt cream

Crème brulée

Ingredients

500ml milk
500ml double cream
130g caster sugar
200g egg yolks
2 vanilla pods, split length ways
250g raspberries, blackberries or
   whimberries (optional)

Serves 6

1 Heat the milk, cream and vanilla pods and leave to infuse for 30 minutes.

2 In a bowl, lightly whisk the egg yolk and 60g sugar until pale, then pour in the cream mixture whisking all the time.

3 Strain into a large jug.

4 Preheat oven to 100°C.

5 Have a large roasting tray ready lined with a tea towel, place gratin or ramekin dishes in the tray. If you are using fruit place in the dishes at this stage then pour in the custard.

6 Place in the oven and pour water around the dishes.

7 Bake for 35 to 40 minutes until set.

8 Remove from the oven and tray and leave to cool, and then transfer to the fridge.

9 Just before serving, sprinkle the tops of the crème brulée with 70g sugar and caramelize with a blowtorch or under a very hot grill, to make a thin pale nut-brown topping.

Coffee

These days coffee shops are on every street corner with the chains such as Café Nero, Starbucks, Prêt and Costa and boy can they charge! When you are on the continent coffee is a way of life. A small strong shot of espresso to keep you going through the day has been the norm for many years. This country for the last 10 years has been catching up with the American way with these trendy cafes but unfortunately this might be to the expense of the greasy spoon type of café, like the ones that filled the valleys of South Wales after the war run by Italians. Now there are very few to be found in the valley where I come from. There are many desserts to be made with coffee such as cakes, mousses and ice creams, but for something really simple try

Coffee granita; all you need is 600ml of very strong coffee, espresso is best, and 120g of caster sugar. Just chill a tray in the freezer in advance, then while the coffee is still hot whisk in the sugar, cool completely and then pour into the chilled tray. Put into the freezer and after an hour give it a stir and continue in half hour intervals using a fork to create coffee crystals. Tip into a plastic container and store in the freezer until ready to serve.

Cappuccino brulée

I first came across the cappuccino brulée at the Ivy restaurant in London and eventually managed to get the recipe. To make this Brulée you will need to make some pastry cream first.

Ingredients

6 egg yolks
75g sugar
250ml cream
250ml milk
25g ground coffee
200ml pastry cream
100ml extra double cream

Serves 6

1 Heat the milk and cream with the coffee.

2 Mix the egg yolks and sugar together and pour the coffee milk over and mix well.

3 Strain through a very fine sieve two to three times to remove all the grains of coffee.

4 Pour into small ramekins or coffee cups up to two-thirds full.

5 Place in a deep tray, pour water half way up the cups and bake in an oven at 150°C for 30 minutes, then check regularly until set, chill in the fridge.

6 When ready to serve take the pastry cream and lightly whip the double cream, mix together.

7 Spoon on top of the baked coffee custard, then cover with a thin layer of brown sugar and caramelize with a blow torch.

For the Pastry cream

Ingredients

3 egg yolks
75g caster sugar
25g plain flour
250ml milk
1 vanilla pod, split lengthways

Serves 4

1 Infuse the vanilla pod in the milk over a low heat for 30 minutes.

2 In a large bowl put the egg yolks together with the sugar and flour, mix well.

3 Pour the hot milk over and put the whole lot back into the saucepan.

4 Over a medium heat and stirring with a wooden spoon simmer the cream until it becomes thick and boils slightly. Don't worry the cream will not separate, the flour prevent it.

5 Strain through a sieve into a clean bowl, cover and leave to cool.

Strawberries

Strawberries are officially in season from late May though to mid July, but there will always be someone around who has not realised that they are meant to be ripe, juicy and sweet and not boring, plastic and tasteless.

A good strawberry is studded with tiny seeds that crunch against your teeth, and should have the wonderful evocative smell that prompted the Romans to call them fraga, for their fragrance. Find strawberries that are good, at farmers' markets and strawberry friendly supermarkets, then just eat them unsweetened out of your hand. Once you have bought your strawberries I would recommend storing them on a tray lined with a paper towel but not in the refrigerator. If your strawberries are inferior, try sprinkling them with a little sugar, a dash of brandy and a few grinds of black pepper. Leave them to macerate for a few hours and serve with tangy yoghurt.

As you may have gathered, I am a man of simple tastes and not one for messing around with food for the sake of invention. One dish that is impossible to improve on is Eton Mess. According to Robin Weir, in *Recipes from the Dairy*, Eton Mess was served in the 1930s in the school's tuck shop, and was originally made with either strawberries or bananas mixed with ice cream or cream. Meringue was a later addition. Other research says that it was served traditionally on the playing fields of Eton with a picnic after the annual prize giving ceremony which takes place in June. Nowadays Eton Mess consists of pieces of crisp meringue, lightly whipped cream and strawberries; all stirred together – hence the name 'mess' which makes it a memorable summer pudding.

Eton mess

Ingredients

1 kg of strawberries
4 meringue shells
300ml double cream
60g icing sugar

Serves 4

1 You will need to make your meringues a day or so in advance or buy them from a supermarket.

2 Cut the strawberries in half or quarters, take approximately 400g of strawberries together with the icing sugar and purée in a liquidiser, then strain through a fine sieve into a clean bowl.

3 Whip the cream to a soft peak. In a large bowl put the remaining strawberries together with the meringues slightly broken up.

4 Fold in the cream and chill in the fridge for 10 minutes or more.

5 Either serve in a glass bowl with the sauce on the side for everyone to help themselves or arrange in the centre of the plate with the sauce poured around.

For the meringues

Ingredients

200g egg whites
400g caster sugar
2 tablespoons of white wine vinegar
2 tablespoons of corn flour

1 Whip the egg whites to a soft peak, then whilst continuing to whip slowly add the caster sugar in a slow stream.

2 When stiff, mix in the vinegar and corn flour.

3 Pipe or spoon onto a baking tray lined with baking parchment paper.

4 Baked for 1 hour at 120°C until they lift off the paper with ease.

5 Store in an airtight container.

Hot puddings

The British have a long and good reputation for dishes like a Steamed Chocolate Sponge, Spotted Dick, Apple Crumble and Jam Roly-Poly, all served with lashings of hot custard.

One great classic is Sticky Toffee Pudding, which must be the most copied pudding. Although it can vary from a half-decent supermarket version to some awful ones found in pubs and restaurants made by people who have probably never read the original recipe. Sticky Toffee Pudding was invented by the late and great chef Francis Coulson of Sharrow Bay in the English Lake District. During the 80s I was lucky enough to have eaten his original pudding, which as the years and lighter tastes emerged, was renamed Sticky Toffee Sponge. While there you always had it, even if you did not order it, and it was pure bliss.

One I must not leave out is Rice Pudding. It's so easy to make as long as you can wait the three hours it takes to cook and, even cold, it's delicious and can be made into many elaborate desserts.

Steamed Ginger Pudding has been a firm favourite on my menus for many years, so much so that a Canadian couple would phone the restaurant at least once a month, always for a Thursday reservation, and make sure it was on the menu. They would then devour it after eating foie gras and roasted duck, so they prove my point.

Rice pudding

Ingredients

75g pudding rice
60g unsalted butter
85g sugar
1 litre milk
300ml double cream
1 vanilla pod, split lengthways
Pinch of salt

1 Put all the ingredients in a shallow pan or baking dish and bake for 3 ½ hours in a low oven at about 150°C. I like it to form a skin on the pudding but if you don't, cover with foil, leave to cool for a while and serve warm.

steamed ginger pudding

Ingredients

100g plain flour
2 teaspoons ground ginger
2 teaspoons mixed spice
1 teaspoon baking powder
1 teaspoon bicarbonate of soda
100g suet
100g fresh breadcrumbs
165g jar preserved stem ginger
200ml milk
50g golden syrup
75g treacle
A pinch of salt
Butter

Serves 6

1 Sieve the flour into a mixing bowl with the spices and raising agents. Add the suet and breadcrumbs and mix well.

2 Coarsely chop the stem ginger; and its syrup in a food processor.

3 Warm the milk with half the stem ginger and syrup, treacle and the golden syrup and a pinch of salt.

4 Beat into the dry ingredients until sloppy, add the salt and mix well.

5 Generously grease a 1 litre pudding basin or six individual moulds with butter and put the remaining stem ginger and syrup in the bottom.

6 Pour in the pudding mixture, cover with buttered foil and steam for 2 hours or 1 hour for the small ones. You can reheat this pudding in the microwave if you wish.

Lemons

Lemons have many uses in the kitchen, and I have always considered them to be the cook's great seasoners, whether adding zing to a butter sauce, enlivening a simple salad, curiously sweetening the bitterness of a dish of braised chicory or correcting the balance of the emulsion of egg and oil in mayonnaise. I love to marinate legs of lamb, either whole or cut into steaks, with the zest and juice of lemons, together with olive oil and garlic. A plain breast of chicken springs to life with some grated garlic, lemon and chopped parsley added to the frying pan at the end of the cooking. The Greeks serve a wedge of lemon with their grilled steaks and, of course, we all squeeze a lemon over our fish. While salt is the essential taste and flavour enhancer in all of these preparations, it is often that elusive sharpening of lemon juice which can joyously bring everything together.

Lemons play a big part in desserts and, in my early days of cooking, a lemon dessert would always feature on the menu. These days a simple Lemon Cheesecake, Sorbet or a favourite from the 70s, a Syllabub, are hard to find on menus. During the 90s all top restaurants would serve a classic Lemon Tart. The great chef Marco Pierre White served the best tart, and when he sprinkled the top with icing sugar, and caramelised it with a blow torch, it took it to even greater heights. An easier version is with individual tart cases filled with homemade lemon curd and then topped with bananas. If you do not have a reliable oven I would most certainly recommend this version.

Lemon curd

Ingredients

Zest and juice of 4 lemons
4 eggs
100g caster sugar
80g unsalted butter

1 Simply put all the ingredients into a stainless steel saucepan and stir over a low heat until thick. Put into a bowl to cool down.

Lemon and banana tart

Ingredients

For the pastry

250g plain flour
85g icing sugar
125g butter
Zest of a small lemon
1 small egg

For the filling

200g sugar
4 large eggs
Juice of 2 large lemons and the zest of 1
125ml double cream
2 bananas
100g of caster sugar for caramelizing

Serves 8

1 Sieve the flour and icing sugar, add the butter and work together, add the egg and lemon zest, mix well, cover with cling film and chill for 1 hour.

2 Mix the egg sugar, lemon juice and zest together, then add the cream.

3 Roll out the pastry into a deep flan case or a pasty ring. Let the pastry overlap the edges, line it with foil and fill with baking beans, bake for 15 minutes at 175°C.

4 Remove the foil and beans, strain the filling though a sieve and check the tart case has no holes. If it does use any scraps of pastry to fill them, put the tart back in the oven and reduce the temperature to 110°C. Pour the filling into the case in the oven so that you can fill it as full as possible. Bake for 40 minutes until he tart has a slight wobble, it will set as it cools down.

5 Cut into portions, slice the banana and cover the surface of the tart slices. Sprinkle with caster sugar and caramelize using a blow torch.

Pink grapefruit, orange and Champagne jelly

Ingredients

½ bottle of Champagne (375ml)
250g sugar
6/8 pink grapefruits, segmented
10/12 oranges, segmented, when in season
blood oranges are great for this dish
9 leaves of gelatine
Juice of half a lemon
Juice of one orange

Serves 10

1 Dissolve the sugar in the Champagne with the orange and lemon juice over a very low heat.

2 Soften the gelatine in cold water and add to the Champagne mixture.

3 Lightly oil a terrine and line with cling film.

4 Strain the Champagne mixture through a very fine sieve.

5 Pour a small amount into the terrine to cover and leave in the fridge to set.

6 Have the orange and grapefruit segments in a sieve over a bowl.

7 Carefully lay the orange segments in a line and cover with the jelly, place in the fridge to set and continue with a layer of grapefruit, cover with jelly and leave to set, continue until the terrine is full, and chill over night.

8 To serve: ease the jelly from the terrine, slice into portions and serve surrounded with passion fruit sauce.

Passion fruit sauce

Ingredients

12 passion fruits, which should give you
    250ml of flesh
175ml glass of white wine
½ tablespoon of sugar

1 Purée the passion fruit in a food processor, pass through a sieve and keep a few tablespoonfuls of the seeds to one side.

2 Put the purée in a saucepan with white wine and sugar and reduce by a third, add the seeds back into the sauce.

Pannacotta with raspberries

Pannacotta means boiled cream. If you come across double Jersey cream it would be wonderful in this dessert. It looks quite elegant and is not too sweet or rich to finish off a meal and probably the hardest part is getting them out of the moulds.

Ingredients

150g caster sugar
600ml double cream
150ml milk
2 vanilla pods (optional), split in two
   lengthways
3 leaves of gelatine
2 tablespoons rum
50g icing sugar
3 punnets of raspberries

Serves 6

1 Put the cream, milk and vanilla pod into a large saucepan and slowly bring to the boil. Lower the heat and leave to simmer for 5 minutes.

2 Meanwhile put the gelatine into cold water to soften, and then drain off all the water.

3 Stir in the sugar and rum, allow to dissolve, remove from the heat and slip in the softened gelatine. Stir well and leave to cool.

4 Place six dariole moulds, small soup bowls or glass dishes on a tray and pour the cold cream into the moulds. Refrigerate until set.

5 Pick out some of the best raspberries for garnish, purée the rest with the icing sugar. Pass through a sieve.

6 To serve run a small knife around the moulds, place in a bowl of boiling hot water for 10 seconds turn onto a cold plate and wait for it to go plop out of the mould. It should be very delicate and wobbly. Pour some raspberry sauce around and a few raspberries on top of the sauce.

Peaches

Dessert for Sunday lunch at my Grandma's would either be trifle or peaches and cream, but the peaches would be out of the tin, and the cream would be courtesy of Carnation. Over the years, times change and fresh peaches are no longer the luxury fruit they once were. In fact there is occasionally an abundance of them in the markets and they are so cheap you could buy them by the tray. It's a good way of buying them because those trays with their cardboard nests protect the fruits so well. For a peach is a delicate thing and easily bruised.

If you see white peaches when out shopping, buy some, and cut them in half, winkle out the centre stone and look at the deep red scars the stone leaves behind. There are few things in food that look so beautiful. They make a lovely salad sliced with tomatoes, drizzled with a few drops of lemon juice and olive oil, with a few chopped walnuts and some torn basil leaves scattered over. A great start to a summer lunch. At Tyddyn Llan we have been poaching our white peaches in Champagne and any rejected halves are served in a Knickerbocker Glory. Now there's a trip down memory lane.

Knickerbocker glory

Ingredients

8 cooked peach halves
Vanilla ice cream
1 punnet of raspberries or blackberries
150ml double cream
Mango purée (optional)
Raspberry sauce (50g of raspberries mixed
  with 20g icing sugar and pushed through
  a sieve)

Serves 4

1 Whip the cream to a soft peak.

2 In four elegant glasses, place a quarter piece of peach, a few raspberries, a scoop of ice cream, a little raspberry sauce and mango purée.

3 Continue building until the glass is full, top with a little cream.

Poached peaches in Champagne

Ingredients

6 ripe peaches
½ bottle of Champagne, Cava or sparkling wine
100g sugar
Juice of half a lemon
Juice of half an orange
1 vanilla pod, split length ways

Serves 4

1 Put a large pot of water onto boil, and have a bowl of iced water ready. Cut the peaches in half and remove the stones. Now drop the peaches into the boiling water a few at a time, leave for a few seconds and plunge into the iced water. Repeat with all the peach halves.

2 In a clean saucepan put all the ingredients except the peaches, place on the heat and bring to a gentle simmer, switch off the heat.

3 Using a sharp small knife carefully remove the skin from the peach halves.

4 Put the peach halves into the Champagne syrup and cover the pan with a circle of baking paper. Place on a gentle heat and bring to a simmer for 2 minutes then take off the heat and allow to cool down. Place in a plastic container with a tight fitting lid and store in the fridge. They will keep for up to a week.

5 Serve in bowls with some juice poured over and a scoop of good vanilla ice cream.

Summer pudding

Summer Pudding means a lot of picking of berries to be done, for which a table fork is my most helpful tool. Summer Pudding was a classic waiting to happen. It's a happenstance of nature when two or three ingredients, in this case raspberries, redcurrants and blackcurrants, coincide for only a limited time in the year.

People argue about what fruit should go into a Summer Pudding, and whether or not the fruit should be cooked. I prefer to cook the fruit. The one fruit that should not be in the pudding is strawberries, as these are now out of season. But redcurrants, blackcurrant, blackberries and whimberries can be used, and raspberries are a must. It does not matter if you can not get all the different berries, just make up the amount with the ones you have.

Another concern is the bread. I think you need a good strong white loaf, slightly stale. Buy a whole loaf from your local baker, and ask them to slice it for you. A sliced cotton wool loaf is not ideal but anything is better than brown.

One other note; when you strain the fruits, and after dipping the bread in it to mould the pudding, any juice left over can be churned in an ice cream machine to make a refreshing summer fruit sorbet.

redcurrants, blackcurrants, blackberries, whimberries and raspberries

summer pudding

Ingredients

1 slightly stale loaf of bread sliced
225g redcurrants
225g blackcurrants
225g whimberies
225g raspberries
225g caster sugar

Serves 6 to 8

1 Remove the crusts from the slices of bread.

2 Put all the fruit except the raspberries in a pan with the sugar and bring to a bare simmer, cook for 3 to 4 minutes.

3 Stir in the raspberries and leave to cool.

4 When cool drain through a colander and leave for about an hour.

5 Have ready a pudding basin and dip the bread in the juices and line the basin with the bread making sure that you overlap the edges.

6 Spoon the fruit mixture to fill the mould to the top, cover the top with the overlapping pieces and, if there is a gap, dip an extra piece of bread to cover the top.

7 Place a small plate on top and put some weights (about a kilo) on top using tins, place in the fridge overnight.

8 You can leave the pudding in the fridge for a couple of days which actually improves the flavour.

9 To serve turn out on to a plate and cut into wedges, serve with some lightly whipped cream and the sorbet if you made it.

Tiramisu

The Italians love sweet things but they seem to pick at little cakes, biscuits and the odd ice cream throughout the day while they sip their espresso, rather than have a dessert at the end of the meal. After a starter, pasta, main course and maybe some cheese, the Italians like a piece of ripe fruit – a pear would be perfect. The one dessert I like that is Italian is Tiramisu which means 'pick me up', although I have tasted some versions in this country which would 'knock you out' with the amount of alcohol used in making it.

All the regions of Italy try to claim the credit for the invention of Tiramisu. The Piedmontese point to the sponge fingers; the natives of Lombardia argue that mascarpone ultimately originates from their country; while the Venetians, Tuscans and Romans regard the dessert as typically Italian, therefore theirs. The only differences of opinion relate to the spirits used. All kinds are possible, from Cognac, Marsala, Amaretto, whisky and rum to coffee liqueur. It's up to your taste. Use what you want to use.

Tiramisu

Ingredients

1 large egg
50g caster sugar
250g tub of mascarpone
1 vanilla pod (optional)
125ml double cream
125ml of espresso
2 tablespoons of rum
2 tablespoons of Tia Maria
2 tablespoons of brandy
Half a packet of sponge fingers
50g of best quality chocolate, grated

Serves 6 to 8

1 Whisk the egg with the sugar until creamy.

2 If using the vanilla, cut the pod in half lengthways, scrape the seeds and mix them with the mascarpone.

3 Whip the cream until it is slightly thick, mix the egg into the mascarpone and then fold in the whipped cream.

4 Mix the coffee and alcohol together in a shallow tray and have ready a dish or stainless tray approximately 1½ cm deep and 20cm x 10cm wide.

5 Quickly dip the fingers in the coffee mix and pack them tightly into the dish, if you have any coffee left over sprinkle over.

6 Spoon the mascarpone on top and leave to chill.

7 Just before serving cover with grated chocolate. I serve simply cut into squares, a fish slice is the best way to get the portions out of the dish.

Biscuit glacé

Ingredients

6 egg whites
375ml double cream
300g sugar

For praline
100g sugar
100g almonds
50g hazelnuts

1 For the praline heat the sugar slowly in a heavy saucepan until it becomes a dark caramel. Add the almonds mix well and pour onto bakewell paper leave to cool. Break into small pieces – this is called praline.

2 Whip the egg whites until firm. Add the sugar to form a meringue.

3 Whip the cream and gently fold the meringue into the cream, adding the praline as you go.

4 Pour into moulds and freeze until needed.

5 Good served with raspberries and raspberry sauce as in the pannacotta (see page 173).

Naughty bits

One of the things that both Susan and I missed when we first moved to North Wales from the metropolitan city of London was being able to dine at a good Thai, Chinese or Indian restaurant whenever we wanted to. Opposite Hilaire on the Old Brompton Road was one of the best kebab shops around (and they tasted just as good sober as they did after a few glasses of wine).

The nearest that I have come to the flavours of that kebab shop in Wales are our great butcher Haydn's burgers, cooked on a griddle pan and served in some toasted pitta bread with fresh crunchy salad and a few dollops of Pain chilli sauce. They're magic after a hard day and when you are in need of some different flavours.

I am pretty boring when it come to eating authentically and always go for the same dishes. With Chinese food it's always something with a black bean sauce; with Indian it's a Sag or Rogan Gosh, although with Thai food I try most things as it's the country I have visited the most, though, as I've mentioned before, we can never pass on a chicken and coconut soup.

Beef with black bean sauce

Ingredients

2 small onions, halved and thinly sliced

2 red peppers, seeds removed, halved and thinly sliced

2 cloves of garlic, peeled and thinly sliced

Sunflower oil

400g of beef, thinly sliced

2 tablespoons of dry sherry

2 tablespoon of light Soya sauce

½ teaspoon of corn flour

1 tablespoon of black bean sauce

4 tablespoons of chicken stock or water

1 large red chilli, finely chopped (leave the seeds in if you want it hot)

1 tablespoon of chopped spring onions

Chopped coriander

Serves 4

This is a staple staff meal dinner; I usually make it when I have enough trimmings of the whole fillets of Welsh Black beef that we buy.

1 In a saucepan slowly cook the onions, peppers and garlic until soft but no colour.

2 Mix the corn flour with one tablespoon of Soya sauce.

3 Heat a large frying pan with some oil until very hot, seal the beef and remove to a tray, season with the remaining Soya sauce.

4 Add the sherry, chicken stock and black bean sauce to the pan; add the Soya and corn flour mix and the cooked peppers bring to a simmer.

5 Add the beef, chilli, spring onions and coriander, mix well and serve.

Cassoulet

Cassoulet is a wonderful dish for cold winter days. It's at the top of my list of favourite dishes to eat and cook. It's more in the style of bistro cooking, and great to serve at home. It's best done the day before so all you have to do is reheat the pot, carry it straight to the table and serve. It will take a long time to prepare but it will be well worth it.

Be careful when buying the haricot beans, making sure that they have a long shelf life as, if old, they will be tough and take forever to cook. You will also need to soak the beans overnight before cooking. When cooking dried vegetables such as beans, chick peas and lentils, do not add any salt until they are cooked.

Wonderful dish for cold winter days

Cassoulet

Ingredients

2kg of pork shoulder diced, save any bone

A piece of pork rind

4 duck legs which have been made into confit
  (see page 63)

4 good Toulouse sausages or any good quality
  garlic flavoured sausage

500g haricot beans, soaked overnight.

1 jar of passata

1 bouquet garni

1 large onion, chopped

2 carrots, peeled and chopped

2 sticks of celery

1 bulb of garlic, peeled (about 8 cloves)

Sunflower oil

Glass of white wine (125ml)

30g of homemade breadcrumbs
  (optional)

Salt and pepper

Serves 8

1 In a casserole dish heat some oil and fry the pork in small batches until well coloured, season with salt and pepper. Remove to a tray.

2 Once all the pork has been sealed add the chopped vegetables and cook until they start to colour. Return the meat add the bone and pork rind and pour over a glass of white wine, add the passata and bouquet garni and cover with water and bring to the boil. Skim off any scum and simmer until cooked; about one hour.

3 Drain the juice into a clean saucepan, put the beans and garlic into the juice with the pork rind, cover with a lid and cook in a oven at 170°C for about 4 hours but check regularly in case the juice boils dry. Cover the meat with cling film.

4 Once the beans are cooked add the pork to the beans, discard the rind and bones and leave to cool.

5 To assemble, cook the sausages gently and cut into chunky pieces, take the meat off the duck legs then using a large casserole dish, put in the pork, beans and sauce, together with the sausage and duck; mix well.

6 Pre heat the oven to 170°C, place the Cassoulet in the oven with a lid on for 30 minutes, remove lid and sprinkle over some breadcrumbs and bake until golden brown. Serve in the pot with a green salad and let the guests help themselves.

Chilli con carne

Chilli con Carne always reminds me of a skiing holiday in Whistler when, at lunchtime in the restaurant on the top of the mountain, they would serve a good warming chilli.

Chilli con Carne was created in Texas during the 1870s as an interpretation of Mexican cuisine. Mexicans, however, deny any part in the creation of the dish and anyone who has travelled to Mexico will testify to its non-existence on restaurant menus. Nevertheless I love it, especially when my wife serves it in taco shells and potato skins with guacamole and sour cream.

Chilli con carne

Ingredients

1 kg minced beef, preferably Welsh Black
1 onion
1 large carrot
1 stick of celery
300g passata
1 to 2 teaspoons dried chilli
100ml white wine
1 tin of red kidney beans, drained
Salt and pepper

Serves 4

1 Heat a large pan and fry off the mince until golden brown, season with salt and pepper and remove to a plate.

2 Chop the vegetables finely; you can cheat by using a food processor.

3 Fry the chopped vegetables, add the meat back to the pan.

4 Add a small glass of white wine and the passata, bring to a boil for a few minutes, cover with water and simmer for 1 hour, add the beans and cook for a further 10 minutes.

5 Serve as you wish with plain rice, pitta bread or taco shells.

Lamb curry

Ingredients

1 piece of ginger about 2½cm, peeled
   and finely chopped

4 cloves of garlic, chopped

2 onions, finely chopped

800g of lamb from the shoulder, diced into
   2½cm cubes

8 cardamom pods

4 cloves

1 teaspoon of cumin seeds

1 teaspoon of coriander seeds

1 teaspoon of crushed dried chilli

1 stick of cinnamon

300g plain yoghurt

4 tablespoon of tomato pasata

Fresh coriander, roughly chopped

Salt and pepper

Sunflower oil

Serves 4

1 Put the dried spices in a clean frying pan and toast them over a low heat for a few minutes, or put in hot oven so that they begin to release their flavours. Grind in a coffee grinder or in a pestle and mortar.

2 Heat a saucepan with sunflower oil, when hot seal the cubes of lamb until brown, season with salt and pepper and remove to a tray. Continue in batches until all the meat is sealed.

3 Add a little more oil and cook the onions for about 6 minutes until lightly coloured, add the garlic and ginger and cook for a few more minutes. Now add the ground spices and stir well, cook for two minutes, then add the meat back to the pan and stir well to coat the cubes of meat with the onions and spices.

4 Add the yoghurt a little at a time, stirring all the time. Once you have added all the yoghurt add the tomato passata, mix well and cover with water, slowly braise for about 1 hour until the meat is tender and the sauce slightly thick.

5 Add the fresh coriander just before serving.

Meat balls

There used to be a Swedish restaurant in London that served fantastic meatballs with a fruity sauce on the side. They are so easy and cheap to make at home and you can serve them in so many ways; in a rich Italian tomato sauce with pasta and fresh Parmesan; with some creamy mashed potatoes; or even make them dinner party style with artichokes and olives.

make them dinner party style with artichokes and olives

Meat balls with artichokes, olives and sage

Ingredients

Olive oil

2 onions, finely chopped

1 kg of minced lamb or veal

Salt and pepper

3 tablespoons of chopped flat parsley

3 tablespoons of freshly grated Parmesan

3 large eggs

75g fresh breadcrumbs

16 small artichokes

About 32 small cherry tomatoes

4 cloves of garlic

20 green olives with the stones removed

2 tablespoons of roughly chopped sage

2 tablespoons of lemon juice

500ml of chicken stock

Serves 4

1 With a generous amount of olive oil slowly cook the onions with some salt and pepper until very soft. This will take about ten minutes.

2 In a large bowl put the mince, parsley, Parmesan, eggs, breadcrumbs and about two-thirds of the onions once they have cooled down.

3 Season with salt and pepper, mix well and form into balls. Pop them into the fridge to firm up, while you prepare the artichokes.

4 In a large frying pan add a little oil and fry the balls until golden brown, place into a baking dish with the remaining onions, fry the artichoke pieces in the same pan and add to the meat balls.

5 Pre heat the oven to 175°C.

6 Gently fry the garlic for 1 minute just to take the rawness away, add the tomatoes, olives, lemon juice and sage, mix well and distribute around the meat balls. Bring the chicken stock to the boil and pour over, tightly cover with foil and bake for about 45 minutes.

7 Serve with mashed potato or creamed polenta.

To prepare artichokes

Have you ever wondered how to cook an artichoke? You can just boil the large ones in salted water, leave to cool and serve with a good bowl of vinaigrette then slowly eat your way through it. Very 70s! Or you can cut the vegetable down to just the heart (really you need to be shown this, were you tear away the outer leaves) then cut away until you just have the centre then cook it and finally pull out the choke. For the meat ball dish buy baby artichokes. In a large pot of salted water cook for about 10 minutes until you can just pull an outer leaf off, cool down. Then peel off the outer leaves and cut the stalk about 5cm from the base. If the stalk seems stringy, scrape away the outer layer, then cut the top tough part of the cone and slice the artichoke lengthways into eights and remove any choke.

A word of warning when holding raw artichoke do not lick your finger or taste anything with your fingers as everything will taste horrid.

Steak and kidney

Susan and I love eating out in restaurants, and giving dinner parties to friends, but it's very rare for us to be invited out to someone's home for dinner, unless it's friends in the trade. It's because people are afraid to cook for a chef. When I go out I just want to relax, enjoy the company with a few glasses of wine and have something to eat, but people can try so hard. Simple is best, though I would not go as far as beans on toast as my wife likes to joke, but I do love a steak and kidney pie or pudding.

Around the country people finish their pies with different pastries – shortcrust, puff, flaky or suet. Some pies are thickened with flour; some contain Worcestershire sauce, mushrooms or vegetables. You may have your own favourite recipe, but this one might make you think "Ah, I have not made one for a while". In winter, what could be better for supper?

I have seen recipes where a combination of steak, kidneys, onions, water and Worcestershire sauce is all mixed, topped with pastry and baked for two-and-a-half hours, but I have never been able to understand or accept that method. It's purely cooking by chance. It is far better to make the stew in advance, so you can season it and get the right flavours, texture and depth to the stew, before covering it with the pastry.

These days you can buy very good quality puff pastry, or else try this easy shortcrust method: put 250g plain flour and 160g butter in a food processor and work into fine crumbs. Add an egg and a teaspoon of milk and make into a dough, but do not overwork. Wrap in cling film and use within a day.

steak and kidney pie

Ingredients

1kg stewing steak

8 lambs kidneys

1 onion, finely chopped

2 carrots, diced

2 sticks of celery, diced

A bouquet garni of thyme, parsley stalks,
    and bay leaves

300ml red wine

300ml chicken stock

Oil for frying

25g butter

25g flour and 25g butter; optional

Puff or shortcrust pastry

Egg wash

Salt and pepper

Serves 4

1 In a large saucepan, heat the oil and when hot, fry the cubes of beef until golden brown, season with salt and pepper. Remove onto a tray. You might need to do this in a few batches.

2 Add 25g of butter and cook the onions, carrots and celery until soft and start to colour.

3 Pour in the red wine and allow to boil, add the meat and cover with the stock and if needed water. Add the bouquet garni and slowly cook for about 1 ½ hours until the meat is tender.

4 Cut the kidneys in half, remove the core and cut each half into three. Heat a frying pan, add a little oil and fry the kidney until golden brown, season with salt and pepper and add to the stew.

5 At this stage you may need to thicken the juices, drain the stew through a colander into a clean saucepan, bring the sauce to the boil, mix the flour and butter together and add to the sauce a little at a time, you may not need it all, it depends on how thick you want the sauce. Add the steak and kidney back into the sauce but discard the bouquet garni.

6 Check the seasoning, and leave to cool, this can be done a day in advance.

7 Put the mix into a large pie dish, roll out the pastry, egg wash the edge and place over the dish, make a hole in the centre and brush with the egg. Bake at 175°C for about 45 minutes. Serve with mashed potato and buttered cabbage.

A bit on the side

Chips

I had not cooked chips in a professional kitchen since my very early days at the Crown at Whitebrook when Mrs Blech would cook them in a chip pan just like my mum, I love chips and I know they are supposed to be no good for you but once a week surely does not hurt. Stepping into the Kitchen at Hilaire a few days before I was to take over, Peter Gordon, the second chef who helped me at lot when I first started, was showing me around and there in front of me were two large trays of blanched chips ready for the night's service, and since my first service at Hilaire chips have always been served with my steak 'au poivre'.

The secret to a fine chip is the potato. There are a few weeks during the summer when you will be unable to find a suitable potato due to their high sugar content, but to be honest at the same time there are always wonderful new potatoes around such as Jersey Royals and Pembroke.

Chips

Ingredients

4 large Maris Piper potatoes, peeled
Sunflower or vegetable oil
Salt

Serves 4

1 Cut the potatoes on the mandoline or into 1cm chips if using a knife and place in a bowl, put under a tap of running water to remove the starch.

2 Drain the chips and dry on a tea towel. Pre-heat a deep fat fryer with the oil to 150°C.

3 When the chips are completely dry blanch the chips in the oil and test with your finger to see if they are ready. They should give to your touch, which will take about 5 minutes.

4 Drain onto a tray lined with some thick kitchen paper.

5 At this point you can put them into a plastic container in the fridge until required.

6 To serve pre-heat the fryer to 190°C. When hot plunge the blanched chips into the hot oil. Have a large metal bowl ready, once they have turned a golden brown drain them into the bowl. You should hear them hit the bowl so that you know they are crisp, I insist on this. Season with salt and serve.

Gratin Dauphinois

We always serve this classic potato dish with our very good local lamb. The recipe is slightly different, but it's good as you can check the seasoning before it goes into the oven and less time-consuming than layering potatoes with cream as in the traditional method.

Ingredients

750g peeled large potatoes
175ml milk
175ml double cream
1 teaspoon salt
2 small cloves garlic grated
15g grated Parmesan cheese

Serves 4

1 Pre-heat the oven to 180°C. Thinly slice the potatoes on a mandoline (about 2mm thick).

2 Put all the other ingredients in a large wide pan and bring to a simmer, add the sliced potatoes and cook for about 5 minutes by which time the starch in the potatoes will produce a thick creamy mixture.

3 Pour into an oven proof gratin dish, cover with baking parchment paper and baking foil, place this dish in a large deep tray, pour water around and bake in the oven for 1 hour. (If you do not have another large tray don't worry just cook at 160°C for 1½ hours and it will be fine.

4 If you plan to serve straight away take the foil and paper off for the last 20 minutes of cooking or leave to go cold and reheat in the oven or on the bottom shelf of the grill.

Pea mashed potatoes

Ingredients

1kg of King Edward potatoes, peeled and
   cut into similar sizes
250g unsalted butter
50 to 75ml double cream
Salt
300g shelled and cooked peas

Serves 4

1 Boil the potatoes in plenty of salted water
and remove any scum as it raises to the
surface.

2 When just cooked drain though a colander
and place onto the pan in which you just
boiled the potatoes and leave to cool for a
few minutes. Do not allow them to go cold
otherwise it will be very hard to pass them
though the mouli.

3 Push though a potato ricer or mouli into
a clean bowl, slowly add the butter piece by
piece. Bring the cream to the boil and add half
to the potato, put the peas into the rest of the
cream and boil, add the potato to the peas,
check the seasoning and serve.

4 If you don't plan to serve the mash straight
away leave the peas and cream separate until
you reheat. You will need a little extra cream if
you do this.

Onion chutney

I have been making this chutney for more
than twenty years. It keeps really well and
goes with all the different terrines that we
serve. It never seems to work if you try to
make it in smaller quantities.

Ingredients

10 onions, peeled, halved and sliced
½ bottle of red wine
750g sugar
200ml sherry vinegar
100g unsalted butter
Salt and pepper

1 In a large saucepan melt the butter and add
the onions, season with a little salt and pepper
and cook slowly until the onions have broken
down and are slightly coloured. This will take
at least 1 hour.

2 Pour in the wine, sugar and vinegar, bring to
a simmer, skim off the fat and impurities that
rise to the surface.

3 Cook for about 6 hours, in which time it will
become a golden colour and slightly thick.
Leave to cool and store in sterile jars.

4 Good with all cold meats.

Potato pancake

Ingredients

500g potatoes
3 tablespoons milk
3 tablespoons cream
3 whole eggs
4 egg whites
3 tablespoons flour

1 Steam or boil the potatoes and purée through a potato ricer or mash while hot. Leave to cool.

2 Add the flour, cream and milk.

3 Add the whole eggs one by one, stirring with a spoon.

4 Whip the egg whites and gently fold into the mix.

5 To cook the pancakes heat a blinis pan with some sunflower oil until hot, tip out the oil and put a ladle of the mixture into the pan. Leave on the heat for a few seconds and then place under a preheated grill or in the oven until firm to the touch and lightly brown.

6 These pancakes are great with chicken and duck as a main course or topped with smoked salmon or eel and topped with horseradish mousse.

Cucumber salad

Ingredients

1 small cucumber
1 teaspoon salt
1 tablespoon of caster sugar
1 tablespoon of white wine vinegar
1 tablespoon of chopped dill

1 Peel and thinly slice the cucumber, a mandoline is good for this.

2 Mix the sliced cucumber with the salt and put into a colander with a small plate on top, over a bowl to drain for 2 to 3 hours.

3 In a clean bowl mix the sugar, vinegar and dill together, add the cucumber and mix.

4 Place in a plastic tub in the fridge until needed. It goes really well with smoked eel, smoked salmon and gravadlax.

Leek risotto

Ingredients

100g unsalted butter
2 leeks, cleaned and finely cut
4 shallots, finely chopped
150g risotto rice carnaroli or arborio
500ml chicken or vegetable stock
25g Parmesan or more if you like
3 tablespoons cream
Salt and pepper

1 Melt 50g butter in a saucepan; add the leeks, season with salt and pepper, cook until soft. Place in a bowl.

2 In a clean saucepan melt the remaining butter, add the shallots and cook until soft for about 5 minutes but do not colour.

3 Add the rice and continue to cook gently for another 3 to 4 minutes. Season the rice with salt and pepper.

4 Add 250ml of the stock, bring to the boil, stirring all the time. Turn down the heat, when the rice has absorbed the stock add a further 250ml of stock, stir and cook slowly. Check the texture of the rice to see if it will need more stock. It's up to you how much – it depends how much bite you want in the rice. I would add all the remaining stock. The whole operation from raw will take 35 minutes, until the rice grains are just cooked but still a little firm.

5 Tip the risotto into a deep tray, cover with cling film and leave to cool. Refrigerate if you are going to leave it a few hours.

6 When you are ready to serve put the leeks in a saucepan with a little stock, if you have some left, or water, add to the risotto, stir until hot, add as much Parmesan as you wish and the cream. Do not put back on the heat; serve in a deep plate with shaved truffles if available.

Polenta

Ingredients

1 litre of cold water
250g polenta flour
Salt
2 tablespoons of mascarpone
Parmesan – it's up to you how much you add

Serves 8

1 Bring the water to boil in a large pan, add a pinch of salt and slowly pour the polenta into the water, stirring all the time until the mixture is smooth.

2 Slowly cook for about 40 minutes while stirring frequently with a wooden spoon, but be careful as sometimes it can erupt like a volcano and it hurts if it hits you.

3 After this time the polenta will leave the side of the pan. Now is the time to add a large knob of butter or a generous spoon of mascarpone and, of course, loads of Parmesan.

Polenta

I fell in love with polenta after eating it at the River Café in London back in the 80s. When the place first opened I tried to copy its flavours but all I could get my hands on was the instant product. Since then, polenta has appeared on menus in all guises. Of these, I still love plain creamed polenta with loads of Parmesan and sometimes a spoonful of mascarpone. I also like it left to cool with less Parmesan, cut into slices and cooked on a griddle. Finally there is a basic polenta mix, with some Parmesan, chopped onion and bacon lardoons, cooked slowly in butter, drained and added, cooled down in a tray, cut into wedges and deep fried until golden and crisp.

Just like all ingredients such as rice, pasta and flour, you need to find the best polenta flour and Bramata Polenta is an organic mixture of three maize kernels, which give you a grainy deep orange and yellow colour alongside a perfume of simmering corn. It is the best, and readily available in any good deli.

Shallots

The shallot is an essential ingredient in any kitchen, its flavour is more subtle than that of an onion and less harsh than that of garlic. They grow in a cluster of bulbs instead of a single one like the ordinary onion and do not produce a seed. Each shallot has two or more sections and each section may have sections. Their elongated shape makes them easier to peel than onions and they don't have the same overpowering smell or tear-inducing power. Shallots do not leave such a strong odour on the palate as onion or garlic. They rarely grow very large, up to 5cm, although there is a cult for banana shallots (so called because they resemble a small banana) and the flavour and juiciness of their pinky grey layers varies according to variety, soil and climate conditions. The shallot is widely used in French cooking. The French praise them more highly than onions, and their comparatively low water content and distinctive penetrating flavour makes them ideal for delicate sauces and dishes that require a subtle onion garlic flavour such as Bercy; béarnaise; red wine sauce; white butter sauce known as beurre blanc, and finely chopped raw as a part of a good tartare sauce with fresh chervil, tarragon and homemade mayonnaise.

When I was a very young and naive lad working in my first ever job I can still remember with amazement being shown how to chop a shallot and onion, obviously my attempt was a mess and ended up in a stock pot but Mrs Blech showed me the correct way to chop my shallots perfectly.

Take a peeled shallot or onion halve it long ways through the root leaving the root intact; lay the flat side on the chopping board, slice finely from the crown end without going all the way through the root, then slice horizontally through the width of the bulb, and finally slice across the middle, the shallot or onion will then fall apart into neat cubes. Discard the root end as this has a bitter taste, I would not even use it in a stock pot.

shallot and thyme purée

Ingredients

750g peeled and roughly chopped shallots
100g butter
A large sprig of thyme
Salt and pepper

Serves 8

1 On a slow heat melt the butter and add the chopped shallots, sprinkle with a teaspoon of salt, stir well and cover with a lid. Let the shallots melt and break down, stir occasionally to stop them browning.

2 Pick the leaves from the thyme and once the shallots are very soft add the thyme and a generous grinding of white pepper. Check to see if it needs any more salt.

3 Tip the shallots into a colander over a bowl and leave to drain for 5 minutes.

4 Purée in a food processor until smooth, reheat when needed.

Vignole

The perfect accompaniment to the wonderful lamb that we have during late Spring and early Summer is an Italian dish called Vignole which is found on the menus of restaurants in Rome, it's one of the dishes that really gets me excited when I have all the ingredients available to make the dish.

When you can get all these beautiful fresh vegetables, try for yourself this great dish; yes it is time consuming but it is really worth the effort. To be more local to Wales use Carmarthen ham. Serve it as a starter with some grilled toasted garlic country bread and keep the lamb simple with some buttered Jersey Royal potatoes.

perfect with lamb

Vignole

Ingredients

1.5 kg each of peas and broad beans in
   their pods
8 small baby artichokes
2 handfuls of fresh mint
4 table spoons of olive oil
50g of butter
2 medium red onions, peeled and finely
   chopped
1 thick slice of Prosciutto
Sea salt, Maldon or Halen Môn and pepper
8 thin slices of Prosciutto, cut into thin strips
Extra virgin olive oil

Serves 8 as a starter or 12 as a main course accompaniment

1 Shell the peas and broad beans. Blanch
the artichokes whole in boiling salted water
for 10 minutes and cool down. Pick the mint
leaves off the stalks and chop half of them.

2 In a separate pan blanch the broad beans
in unsalted water for 2 minutes.

3 Prepare the artichokes as on page 187.

4 In a large pan, heat two tablespoons of olive
oil with the butter, then gently fry the chopped
onion until lightly brown, add the peas and stir
to coat them. Season with salt and pepper and
barely cover them with water, add the thick
slice of ham and the mint leaves and simmer
until tender.

5 In a separate pan add the olive oil and fry the
artichoke until golden brown. Season and add
to the peas.

6 Remove the slice of ham, add the broad
beans and chopped mint, heat through but
do not boil. Stir in the strips of ham and extra
virgin olive oil.

7 Serve at room temperature with roast lamb
or with bruschetta as a first course.

Braised red cabbage

Ingredients

1 small red cabbage, thinly sliced
1 small onion, finely chopped
50g butter
1 glass red wine (125ml)
2 teaspoons of redcurrant jelly
2 tablespoons red wine vinegar
3 tablespoon of sultanas
Chicken stock
Salt and pepper

Serves 8

1 Melt the butter in a saucepan, add the onion
and cook for five minutes, add the red cabbage
and stir well so that it is coated with the onions
and butter. Season with salt and pepper.

2 Add all the other ingredients and bring to a
gentle simmer, cook for about 5 minutes, add
some stock or water to barely cover, cover with
a lid and cook slowly in a moderate oven or
over a low heat until there is only a slight bite
to the cabbage.

Wild garlic

Wild garlic is very common in Wales and other parts of the UK. The native bulb seems to thrive in dark and damp patches of ground near streams or lakes, but I have also noticed it growing happily as a natural border in the shade of the dry stone walls that keep the sheep in and line the narrow roads. Down by the water you will find it in shady patches, rudely poking its white flowers in between the banks of bluebells, forcing a colourful contrast upon that altogether gentler scented spring bloom.

My salad grower from Harlech picks it for me, but one early spring while visiting a chef friend Jeremy in Scotland, we went out to pick wild garlic; some for his menu and a few carrier bags for me. But beware, on long journeys home the smell will overpower your car and the odour will linger for weeks!

Wild garlic bubble and squeak

Ingredients

500g cooked dry mashed potatoes
1 small onion finely chopped
200g wild garlic leaves
75g butter
100g dry cured bacon
Parsley
¼ spring cabbage
Salt and pepper

Serves 8 as a starter

1 Melt the butter and slowly cook the onion until very soft and with no colour.

2 Cut the bacon into fine strips and fry until lightly coloured add to the onions.

3 In a pan of boiling water blanch the garlic. If there are any thick stems remove them, chop the cabbage and boil in the same water, drain and cool down. Squeeze dry.

4 Drain the cooked onion of the butter and in a large bowl put the potato, onion, bacon, garlic and cabbage. Mix well, chop the parsley and add to the mix, season with salt and pepper.

5 Shape into small round cakes. At this point you can shallow fry the cakes or cover in flour, eggs and breadcrumbs and deep fry. Serve as a starter or with grilled slices of calves liver as a main.

Courgettes

Courgettes are available all year round, but summer is when they are at their best. At Tyddyn Llan we serve an array of seasonal vegetables with the main courses of our Sunday lunches, and courgette 'frites' go down very well.

Deep fried courgettes

Ingredients

4 medium size courgettes
A handful of flour
2 large eggs
3 tablespoon milk
Fine breadcrumbs
Sunflower oil for frying
Salt

Serves 4

1 Cut the top and bottoms off the courgettes and slice thinly.

2 Mix the milk and eggs together.

3 Take three large bowls, put the egg, flour and breadcrumbs in each one separately.

4 Coat the courgettes in the flour, then dip the courgettes in the egg, lift out with your fingers and toss in the breadcrumbs so that they are evenly covered.

5 Heat the oil to 190°C, preferably using a deep fat fryer, fry the courgettes until a light golden brown, season with salt and serve straight away.

The basics

Fish sauce and its variations

Ingredients

700g – 1kg of fish bones, the weight is
   approximate
1 chopped onion
1 leek, cleaned and chopped
1 bulb of fennel, chopped
2 sticks of celery, chopped
2 bay leaves, a sprig of thyme and a sprig
   of parsley or just the stalks.
75g butter
125ml glass of dry white wine
125ml glass of dry Martini or Noilly Prat
300ml double cream

1 This is my way of making a stock and basic sauce all in one. Melt the butter in a large pan and add all the vegetables, slowly cook until soft.

2 Add the wines and bring to the boil, add all the bones and cover with cold water.

3 Bring to the boil and skim the scum that rises to the surface.

4 Add the herbs and reduce the heat to a gently simmer for 20 minutes only, any longer and you take the chance of the stock becoming bitter.

5 Strain the stock first through a colander and then through a fine sieve.

6 Reduce the stock by half in a wide pan. At this stage you can leave to cool and freeze in ice-cube trays or use as you wish. Fish stock does not keep in a fridge for longer than two days so it's best to freeze it.

7 To finish off your sauce I would add 300ml of cream to 400ml of fish stock, bring to the boil, being careful it does not boil over and reduce until slightly thick.

8 For a saffron sauce add a few stems and some chopped tomatoes. For mustard sauce simply add mustard and dill if you wish. For watercress sauce add two bunches of the leaves but not too much stalk. Blitz in the food processor and pass through a sieve.

Veal stock

Ingredients

3 kg of veal bones, from the knuckle if possible
2 onions, roughly chopped
4 carrots, roughly chopped
4 sticks of celery, roughly chopped
4 tablespoons of tomato purée
1 bottle of red wine
Large sprig of thyme
8 bay leaves

1 Roast the bones on a spacious tray in a hot oven until golden brown.

2 Tip any fat that melts from the bones into a large saucepan and, over a high heat, add all the chopped vegetables and cook until soft and lightly brown. Add the tomato purée and continue cooking for another 5 minutes.

3 Add half the wine and bring to a gentle simmer. Add all the bones to the pot and pour the rest of the wine into the tray. Scrape from the tray all the goodness left behind from the bones, pour all this into the pot of bones, cover with cold water, bring to the boil and skim the scum and fat that will rise to the surface.

4 Turn down the heat so that it gently simmers, skimming the surface at least every 30 minutes and topping up with cold water when necessary.

5 After 6 hours drain the stock. The best way is to have a colander placed over a large bowl and carefully lift out the bones using a slotted spoon or spider into the colander, with the bowl underneath catching the juices. Continue with this until all the bones are removed, then strain the stock though a fine sieve and add all the juices from the bowl.

6 Cool down overnight, then remove the fats that will have risen and set at the surface, this will keep a week in the fridge or frozen in the freezer for three months.

Add half the wine and bring to a gentle simmer

Chicken stock

Ingredients

3 kg chicken carcasses with all skin and fat removed

4 sticks of celery

3 large carrots

1 leek

2 onions

6 bay leaves

Large sprig of thyme

A small bunch of parsley

1 Put the chicken carcasses in a large saucepan and cover with cold water, bring to the boil and remove all the scum that will rise to the surface. Turn down to a simmer.

2 Peel the vegetables and cut into quarters.

3 After about 20 minutes of the chicken simmering and skimming the surface add the vegetables, after 1 hour add the herbs; continue to cook for about 3 hours in total.

4 Pass though a fine sieve, leave to cool down. It will keep for four days in the fridge or can be frozen for up to three months.

Glacé

This is the basis for the steak au poivre sauce and many types of gravy. It will keep up to two weeks in the fridge or, as you only need a little at a time, you can freeze it in an ice cube tray, then empty it into a freeze bag and keep it in the freezer until needed.

Ingredients

500ml of chicken stock

500ml of veal stock

1 Put both stocks in a large saucepan and bring to the boil, remove the scum and fats that will rise to the surface. It's amazing how much will continue to rise.

2 Reduce over a fairly rapid heat, skimming as it reduces until a slightly thick consistency has been reached, strain though a fine sieve and cool down.

Vinaigrette

Ingredients

500ml olive oil

150ml walnut oil

100ml tarragon vinegar

½ tablespoon mustard

10g salt

A few turns of black pepper

1 Place all the ingredients into a large bowl and mix well with a whisk, check the seasoning and keep in an airtight container.

I always keep some vinaigrette in an empty mineral water bottle with a lid on, so every time you need some just shake the bottle and with your thumb over the neck of the bottle you can control the flow.

Red wine sauce

Ingredients

400ml of a strong full bodied red wine but
not too expensive

400ml veal, beef or chicken stock. Buy it from
a well known supermarket if you don't have
any or the time to make it. It will not work
with a stock cube!

4 shallots, finely chopped

Sprig of thyme, rosemary and a few
parsley stalks

4 bay leaves

2 tablespoons of good red wine vinegar

1 tablespoon of redcurrant jelly

A few peppercorns

1 tablespoon of butter or cream (optional)

1 Put the red wine, shallots, peppercorns and
herbs in a saucepan and over a slow heat
reduce by two-thirds.

2 In a separate saucepan boil the redcurrant
jelly and vinegar for 1 minute and then add to
the red wine reduction.

3 Add the stock and simmer until it starts to
thicken, strain through a fine sieve.

4 Optionally add the cream or butter, boil for a
second and serve.

Lamb jus

Ingredients

1kg of lamb bones and trimmings

125ml glass of white wine

125ml glass of red wine

1 onion, chopped

2 carrots, peeled and chopped

2 stick of celery

1 whole bulb of garlic, cut in half

Parsley stalks, 3 sprigs of thyme and
rosemary

3 bay leaves

600ml of chicken stock

600ml veal stock

1 Brown the bones and trimmings in a
roasting tray in a hot oven.

2 Drain the lamb fat into a large saucepan;
add the onions, carrots, celery and garlic
and cook until lightly brown, pour off any
surplus fat.

3 Add the wine and put the bones into the
pan, bring to the boil and add the thyme, bay
leaves, parsley and tomatoes. Cover with the
stocks and cold water, leave to simmer for 50
minutes, skimming any scum and fat that rises
to the top from time to time.

4 Drain though a sieve and leave to cool,
refrigerate overnight.

5 The next day, remove the layer of fat that will
have formed on the top and discard, pour the
sauce into a clean saucepan and reduce until
slightly thickened.

6 Drain into a clean plastic container and use
with the rack of lamb or the stuffed saddle with
parsley stuffing or a simple roast leg of lamb.

The wine list
by Neville Blech

When Bryan asked me to devise the wine list for Tyddyn Llan, I had to take into consideration three aspects; firstly, the size of the list; secondly the suitability of the list viz á viz Bryan's style of cooking; and thirdly the aspirations of the operation in relation to the market that Tyddyn Llan hoped to attract.

The third consideration was the most difficult, since here we had a kind of hybrid situation, where on the one hand, Bryan and Susan had set out to attract the sophisticated customer from around the world who would be fully appreciative of the cuisine and the country house atmosphere, and on the other hand, a keenness not to lose any good local trade that had been built up by the previous owners.

As usual, some compromises had to be made in considering exactly where to set out one's stall in the market place. Obviously, you couldn't be so expensive by charging London prices for wines, nor could you just have a selection of boring 'pub' wines which most of the other establishments around were selling and all supplied by local suppliers. The lack of wine specialist staff was another consideration as it was certainly not commercially viable to employ a sommelier, but most of the wines listed (with the exception of top Bordeaux and Burgundy wines) could be accompanied by tasting notes to enhance choice selection.

The wine list at Bryan's previous establishment, Hilaire, in South Kensington, London already had, at my instigation, wines listed by style rather than by country, but at the time, I was not fully in charge of its content. This was divided into eight categories. For Tyddyn Llan, therefore, we decided to further refine the categorisation and increase the different styles to 17 in number to reflect a different style or weight of wine; different fruit characteristics, as well as obvious differences

of sweetness and dryness. So we have finished up with eight white, seven red, one dessert and one rosé section. Within each category, except for the half bottles and magnums, the wines have been grouped by country, but not by price. The half bottle and magnum lists are not in any special order as they are smaller.

Another consideration was what would our 'house' wines be? Many establishments just have a 'house' red and a 'house' white – decent enough to drink, but catering for those customers who are only really interested in the cheapest wine on the list and not bothering to explore its contents. At Tyddyn Llan, we decided to have a 'house selection' drawn from one wine in each of the sections; not necessarily the cheapest, but at the less expensive end of the spectrum. All these wines are available by the glass, if desired. We hoped that this would encourage customers to explore the list, by experimenting with wines by the glass from our house selection. Experimentation is also to be encouraged within the various sections. For example, if there is a wine that the customer knows and likes in a particular section, they could try another wine from that section – it would have similar characteristics. This, of course, also applies if a wine happens to be temporarily out of stock.

Nearly all of these wines on the list (with the exception of the Champagnes) are produced by small, dedicated winegrowers, some of whom we have broken bread with ourselves (and opened bottles, too!) and customers are certainly most unlikely to encounter these wines at their local supermarket or high street chain wine shop.

It is always important when making a choice of wine, to look at the sauce as well as the flesh in the dish. Fruity sauces demand fruity wines – dishes with little or no sauces will match wines with complex, dryer flavours better than those with big jammy, upfront fruit. Whilst it may be perfectly agreeable to drink light red wine with fish, it is far more enjoyable to drink white wines which complement the flesh and flavour of fish – lighter, dryer wines with delicate fish, lightly sauced; and richer wines with richer sauces and firmer, fleshy fish. Game goes best with big, powerful wines, whether dry or fruity (depending on the sauce), whilst white meats and poultry can be equally at home with weighty whites as well as light to medium reds.

In an ideal world, it would be wonderful to match each of Bryan's dishes on the menu on any particular day with the various sections in the wine list. Whatever wine appears in a particular section would go equally as well as other wines in that same section. There is therefore only a choice of price to make in that section to suit your budget. Of course an added complication is that some dishes would go with more than one section's wines – it can also be a matter of personal choice as to whether you would drink a medium-bodied or full-bodied wine with beef, for example. In the end, I have taken some of Bryan's signature dishes and matched them with the sections that I think would go best with them and pointing out one or two of my personal favourites.

Griddled scallops with vegetable relish and rocket.

The inherent sweetness of the scallops and the relish is balanced by the crisp acidity of the rocket and this dish would go well with either off-dry to medium wines, fruity, fragrant and aromatic wines or fine rich dry to medium wines. On the current list, my favourites are Conundrum (off-dry to medium),

Albariño Lagar de Cervera (fruity, fragrant and aromatic) and the Lugana Ca' Molin (fine rich dry to medium).

Red mullet with chilli and garlic oil on a bed of spiced aubergine purée

This is a robust dish, the chunky flesh of the red mullet is integrated with the smokiness of the aubergine purée and the spiciness of the chilli and garlic oil. Here, dry and pungent wines, fruity or spicy full-bodied wines and full-bodied dry to medium wines would suit. My favourites in each of these sections with this dish would be Collard's Hawkes Bay Chenin Blanc (dry and pungent), Luna Pinot Grigio (fruity or spicy full-bodied) and Nuits-St-Georges Blanc, Domaine Robert Chevillon (full-bodied dry to medium).

Grilled sewin with asparagus salad

This is a light and delicate dish which would go equally as well with light dry wines as with richer full-bodied wines so really there is a lot of choice here although I think it would be best to avoid wines which are either too sweet or too aggressive. Light, dry white wine Ch. Peyruchet – a grassy Sauvignon from Bordeaux which would certainly suit the asparagus. For a fruity, fragrant and aromatic white wine a 'fat' and fragrant Sancerre Blanc from Gérard Morin, whilst for fine rich dry or full bodied dry to medium dry we have two not dissimilar wines from the old world and the new world – the judiciously oaked Pouilly Fuissé 'Champs Roux' from Jean-Michel Drouin and Warren Winiarski's equally well-crafted Stag's Leap Winecellars 'Karia' Napa Valley Chardonnay 2005.

Roast wild bass with laverbread butter sauce

This dish (or at least the sauce), is a little richer than the last one, so here we would stick to the more full-bodied white wines. The laverbread acts as a streak of acidity cutting through the richness of the beurre blanc, so wines that are more spicy than fruity are the order of the day here. Fruity, spicy full-bodied Piuatti's Estate Vineyard Pinot Grigio 'Le Zuccole' is a good match whilst wines that are a little bit richer such as the fine rich dry to medium dry Chardonnay 'Lidia' from La Spinetta, has enough weight to take the sauce. If you like your wines more full-bodied, then the stunningly sophisticated 'Ovation' Chardonnay from Joseph Phelps is an excellent match, too.

Leg of rabbit with black pudding, Carmarthen ham and mustard sauce

Rabbit flesh is not dissimilar from chicken, but in a more substantial way. The addition of the black pudding and the Carmarthen ham, makes this a pretty trencherman dish, which calls for a pretty big red wine. Nevertheless, the mustard sauce calls for something a little more racy. We have a medium bodied fruity red Cline Cellars California Zinfandel which packs bags of upfront fruit and if you want something a little more substantial then the big scale dry red Chianti Classico from Castello di Ama is a great match.

Osso bucco with saffron rice

One of the great Italian classics, this can be accompanied by lighter wines which are more on the dry side than on the fruity side and here the light, dry red 'Grannero' Pinot Nero from the Terre Rosse Estate has enough finesse even to match with the saffron risotto. This wine is unoaked, as is the slightly heavier medium bodied dry red Mondeuse from Raymond Quenard in Savoie.

Breast of Gressingham duck potato pancake and apple sauce

The sauce here calls for a fruitier wine rather than a dry one and the flesh of the duck would take a fruity full-bodied white as well as a red, so we could choose from a fruity or spicy full bodied white as well as medium bodied and big scale fruity reds. For white, I like Domaine Rieflé's Gewurtztraminer Grand Cru Steinert whilst a medium-bodied fruity red, Joseph Phelps 'Le Mistral' – a Californian Châteauneuf du Pape clone would go equally as well. Slightly heavier, a big scale fruity red Clos de los Siete from Argentina – a blend of Malbec, Cabernet Sauvignon, Merlot and Syrah, has serious upfront fruit even if the wine is made by a Frenchman!

All of the last three dishes would go equally as well with any wines in the smooth and mature wines section. What you choose would depend entirely on your pocket, but I would feel equally at home eating any of these dishes with either the cheapest (Mount Gisborne Pinot Noir, from Victoria in Australia), or the most expensive (Ch. Palmer, a classified third growth from Margaux). Probably the most versatile wine in this section, mainly because of the purity of its fruit, is the Il Rosso di Enrico Vallania Cabernet Sauvignon Cuvée.

I have left out mentioning bubbly, sweet wines and rosé wines. Obviously the sweet wines are there to match the desserts, but the Sémillons (Keith Tulloch Botrytis Sémillon) and the two classic Sauternes, (Ch. Haut Mayne and Ch. Lamothe Giugnard) are also candidates for foie gras and blue cheese and the Gaillac Doux 'Renaissance', fits into this category, too. The Rivesaltes is excellent with pastries and tarts, whilst the Moscato 'Bricco Quaglia' from La Spinetta, with only 5% alcohol is just about as far away as you can get from cheap and nasty Asti. Both the bubbly section and the rosé sections are very versatile, especially with light dishes and obviously very refreshing.

Index